DEMING
AND
GOLDRATT

The Theory of Constraints
and the
System of Profound Knowledge

THE DECALOGUE

DEMING AND GOLDRATT

The Theory of Constraints and the System of Profound Knowledge

THE DECALOGUE

BY
DOMENICO LEPORE
AND
ODED COHEN

The North River Press

Additional copies can be obtained from your
local bookstore or the publisher:

The North River Press
Publishing Corporation
P.O. Box 567
Great Barrington, MA 01230
(800) 486-2665 or (413) 528-0034

www.northriverpress.com

Manufactured in the United States of
America

ISBN 0-88427-163-3

*We dedicate our book to those
who strive to reconcile opinions and
philosophies perceived to be in conflict.*

CONTENTS

DEMING AND GOLDRATT

The Theory of Constraints
and the
System of Profound Knowledge

THE DECALOGUE

Preface

This book is the fruit of four years of collaborative work between Domenico Lepore and Oded Cohen. It started when Domenico, a Dr. W. Edwards Deming scholar, met Oded, a partner of Dr. Eli Goldratt. Their meeting led them to realize that there was much in common between Dr. Deming's Theory of Profound Knowledge (TPK) and Dr. Goldratt's Theory Of Constraints (TOC).

TPK and TOC are systems-based approaches to management, and they both seek out the profound roots that are the origin of the process of ongoing improvement.

Domenico and Oded realized that, while these two theories provided a general framework and a formidable wealth of knowledge, neither supplied sufficiently comprehensive guidelines to help managers lead continuous improvement in the performance of their systems. However, one theory could "complete" the other.

Domenico felt that for those who had started the Deming

journey, TOC offered a methodology and a set of tools consistent with Deming's message. Dr. Deming's theory does not, in fact, provide detailed instructions for implementation. The Thinking Processes Tools of TOC offered a powerful support for day-to-day applications; they provided the methodology for developing implementation procedures as well as gaining consensus.

Oded's interest in Deming's work came from a different angle. In over twenty years with Dr. Goldratt he had been puzzled by the difficulty people often had in comprehending TOC and taking it on board to ensure long-lasting results. Core issues in Deming's philosophy, such as appreciation for a system, understanding variation, process improvement, and so on are not treated explicitly in TOC. It is left to the practitioner to fill the gaps. Becoming familiar with Deming's teachings helped Oded find what was missing in TOC, and how to make it negotiable for many more managers.

What we came to realize in the course of our work was that the overlap between Deming's and Goldratt's approaches was even greater than we initially thought. By creating a link between Deming and Goldratt, we believe we have developed a more comprehensive map to guide and sustain organizations in a continuous improvement pattern. We have called it The Decalogue.

The Decalogue is a ten-step map that brings together all the necessary elements to sustain knowledge-based improvement. By knowledge we mean the knowledge created by understanding our system and the variation that affects it, together with the analysis of cause-effect relations that form the basis of Goldratt's Theory of Constraints. There may be other approaches that bring about improvement, such as the intuitive approach many entrepreneurs adopt, or even the "rule by fear" approach. However, these results tend to be confined to the short to medium term. Only action based on knowledge can provide the foundation for long-term and continuous improvement.

Domenico Lepore
Oded Cohen

For further information see www.thedecalogue.com

Acknowledgments

First, we would like to acknowledge the contribution of the two great men, Dr. Edwards Deming and Dr. Eliyahu Goldratt. Their work inspires and enhances our knowledge, horizons and lives.

Domenico Lepore:

In my quest to understand the teachings of Dr. Deming, I was greatly helped by the work of Henry Neave, who is W. Edwards Deming Professor of Management at the Nottingham Trent University, England, and Dr. Donald Wheeler.

Henry's book, *The Deming Dimension*, represents, in my opinion, the most rigorous, knowledgeable and pleasurable way to begin the Deming Journey. His understanding of Dr. Deming's teachings is unrivaled; the contents of Chapter 5 owes much to his book and to papers developed with the British Deming Association. Henry's criticisms of the first draft of this book, harsh but fair, helped the both of us to focus better on the aim of our work.

Don Wheeler is the man who took the baton from Dr. Deming in the crusade for generating and disseminating knowledge on variation. His numerous publications have made understanding variation possible for everyone. His lessons are masterpieces of clarity and wit. The study of his books has enhanced my professional life as much as Dr. Deming's. I owe him my understanding of the need for stable systems, Statistical Process Control, and its applications. We could not have written Step Three without drawing heavily from him; all his books are mandatory reading for anybody who is serious about process improvement.

I also wish to acknowledge Mrs. Cecelia Kilian's book, *The World of W. Edwards Deming*, for its thorough account of Dr. Deming's life and achievements, and Dr. Brian Joiner's *Fourth Generation Management* for its clarification on how to improve stable and unstable processes.

I would like to say thank you to all our clients, past and present. Without their willingness to work hard to produce results, The Decalogue would have remained a theory. Special thanks go to Raffaele Moneta from Sistemi Quemme; Roberto Secchi and Giuseppe Moccia from Yokogawa Italia; and Gian Piero Barozzi and Tarcisio Mussi from AISA Industries for their enthusiasm and sheer commitment to making The Decalogue happen.

Finally, I am grateful to my wife, Angela, for the quality of our love; a unique case of reliability without predictability.

Oded Cohen:

I would like to thank Dr. Goldratt personally. Our long-term relationship has influenced my career. Since 1977 Eli has been a part of my life as a supplier, a boss, a senior partner, a friend, and more than anything else—my personal mentor.

I must confess that the major reason that I wanted to work with Eli was that I knew that he had this thing called *Thinking Processes*, and I was patient enough to wait until 1985 when the work started and until 1995 when the Thinking Processes had been brought to a "good enough" level—so that we could continue and develop more knowledge using the tools we have.

The Thinking Processes is the biggest gift I got from Eli. In our tradition the best way to give a reward for a gift is to give the gift to others. My goal is to continue to develop TOC and convey it to others. Thank you, Eli.

I also would like to thank everyone who has helped and assisted me in the long quest for knowledge and TOC. Without the understanding and active support of my family, I couldn't have made it. Their willingness to accept a husband and a father who is closer to a Marco Polo rather then a regular house inhabitant is appreciated. In addition, I would like to thank: my team in the U.K. headquarters who have helped with advice and input to the written material; my network, the associates of the Goldratt Institute, for their long-term standing in the odyssey to bring TOC to a challenging market like the U.K.; and all my students, the "Jonahs", who have been courageous in implementing TOC in their organizations and who have been honest and open in sharing their thoughts and concerns.

We both want to thank the team who helped us make this book happen:

Chiara Ferrarotti for consolidating our work and for bridging it into a better style; Angela Montgomery for translating our Anglo-Hebrew-Italian jargon into proper English (and coping with the idea of American spelling); Barbara Zenoni for contributing to the development of The Decalogue and making it happen; Claudio Vettor for contributing to the growth of mst in Italy; Sara Baroni, who has based on The Decalogue her research work at the Department of Mechanical Engineering, University of Brescia; and Cia Elkin and Larry Gadd at North River Press for believing in The Decalogue. Their vision, continuous support, and encouragement have made this book possible.

Introduction

We wrote this book to satisfy a need.

That need is to manage effectively. That means being able to obtain results within the context of a process of continuous improvement. We will call this goal the "Quality Project." Why is it such a problem to achieve effective management within a process of continuous improvement? Because the assumptions underlying our management methods spring from a world view or paradigm that does not match our needs. What are these assumptions, and what is this world view?

- A vision of an organization that is hierarchical and not systemic
- The pursuit of local optimization at the expense of global optimization
- A management approach oriented toward the "cost reduction world" rather than the "increasing performance world"

These assumptions have been challenged by both W. Edwards Deming and Eliyahu M. Goldratt. Their ideas are a fundamental contribution to the Quality Project. Up to now their teachings have generally been used separately. We believe that together they provide the direction and the tools to make continuous improvement work. (A brief profile of their lives, work and achievements can be found in Chapter 5.)

Deming's philosophy involves a radical rethinking of our conception of company management. It requires a cross-cultural approach and profound knowledge of areas that differ greatly from one another. A company that is determined to create Quality has to foster the understanding that an organization is a system.* It has to encourage people to study effects in order to find their root causes. It gears itself toward examining processes instead of simply concentrating on results.

From a purely philosophical point of view, for Deming the goal of Quality is profound knowledge of the impact actions have on a system as a whole. In other words, achieving Quality means the ability to anticipate the development of events and thus have greater control over them. Indeed, the ability to predict events is one of the major elements of profound knowledge in Deming's approach to management.

What is the major factor that prevents us from predicting? It is variation.

If we do not understand the variation of processes, we cannot assess how our actions to improve things impact other parts of the system. We always have to remember that the processes that make up a system are interdependent. We can achieve maximum Quality through minimum variation in processes.

In spite of their power, in too many cases the application of these principles has been disappointing. If we are convinced of the value of Deming's work, we need to know which obstacles

---

* The term *Quality* was brought into management by Walter Shewhart on May 16, 1924. Quality was a key concept of Deming. To denote its importance, we use the term with a capital *Q*.

stand in the way of our achieving concrete results, and we need to have the right tools to overcome these obstacles.

A major input comes from the Theory of Constraints—TOC—developed by Eli Goldratt. TOC looks at an organization as a chain of interdependent processes. TOC aims at achieving the goal of a system or organization by focusing on the weakest link in the chain—the constraint. This is done with the aid of logical tools called Thinking Processes.

How can TOC help us apply Deming's ideas?

The tools of TOC provide the necessary focus to initiate and sustain the continuous improvement process.

In order to bring about a Quality project we must first address these three questions:

- What to change?
- What to change to?
- How can we make the change possible?

The first question is, what to change? When we start a Quality project we face a series of problems. For instance:

- Feeling we do not have control over the situation
- Knowing we can do more but not knowing how
- Having managers who aren't pro-active enough
- Experiencing symptoms that internal procedures and work methods need re-examining

These problems are not unrelated. TOC claims that they all stem from a common source. We call this source *the constraint*. In this case the constraint is our inability to deal with problems satisfactorily when we manage change.

The second question is, what to change to? This involves developing a practical solution to deal with the constraint. To do this, we need an innovative idea that dictates the direction of the change. This will be found in the approach we put forward in this book: the Ten Steps (The Decalogue), which combines Deming's philosophy with Goldratt's Theory of Constraints.

THE DECALOGUE

STEP ONE
Establish the goal of the system, the units of measurement and the operating measurements

STEP TWO
Understanding the system

STEP THREE
Making the system stable

STEP FOUR
Identify the constraint and carry out the Five Focusing Steps

STEP FIVE
Implementing buffer management

STEP SIX
Reduce the variability of the constraints and the main processes

STEP SEVEN
Creating a suitable management structure

STEP EIGHT
Eliminate the external constraint: selling the excess capacity

STEP NINE
Bringing the constraint inside the organization when possible

STEP TEN
Set up a continuous learning program

By following these Ten Steps we not only set the direction, but we also answer the third question, which is, how can we make the change possible?

The goal of this book is to provide a path to follow: how to deal with the constraint that prevents us from achieving continuous improvement in our organizations.

Chapter 1

Getting Started

The First Three Steps of The Decalogue

It would be better if everyone would work together as a system, with the aim for everybody to win.
—W. Edwards Deming (1)

Written into our DNA somewhere is the quest for happiness and a better life. We are all aware, although to differing degrees, that for ourselves and others, things could be better than they actually are, that we can do more to obtain that better life.

People who have positions of responsibility within organizations feel this even more urgently. They know what it means to suffer the negative effects of not knowing how to react and adapt to change.

Many of these people in trying to bring about improvement in line with the changes going on around them, experience the terrible frustration of their failures, or of their very minor successes.

The root cause of this situation is the prevailing culture in the Western world: *competitiveness* in all fields and at every level. The competitive spirit is hailed as the engine of economic life. It is considered a fundamental aspect of the growth and development of individuals and organizations. It is considered indispensable for improvement.

But reality shows that not only does a competition-based culture fail to deliver the hoped-for benefits, it actually impedes every attempt at real innovation and effective improvement.

The negative effects of our competition based management methods are sadly evident both in individuals and organizations.

We have to find a solution.

The "how" in how we manage our organizations has to be radically transformed. Our goal must be a way of behaving and working that allows everyone to win. Management based on cooperation not competition.

If we really succeed in thinking and adopting a management approach that allows us to improve the quality of what we produce, then we can spark off the chain reaction that Deming described.

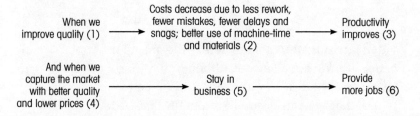

It is time for us to understand that we are better off when we live and work as a system.

What this transformation requires is a true revolution in our way of thinking and behaving. But we cannot get away with simply changing our outward behavior or our corporate image. We are talking about a change that deeply affects the way each one of us sees the world.

In every organization we face the problem of transforming the strategies we have defined into a successful operational plan.

The reason why many new initiatives fail is that they conflict with our view of reality.

These conflicts are often generated by the hidden assumptions that lie behind our way of thinking. For this reason, if we want to change our approach to managing organizations we must bring these assumptions to the surface.

If we can come to understand the existence of these "mental models," and we decide to challenge them, we will have acquired an essential tool for reacting to the relentless changes in the reality we are in.*

We have to get used to thinking that we are part of a system and to understanding exactly what this means.

STEP ONE
Establish the goal of the system, the units of measurement and the operating measurements

What is a system?

We can define a system as a network of interdependent components, which work together to achieve the goal of the system.

Let's look at this definition in detail. This will help us understand what it means to be a manager. It will also point to the actions we have to take to achieve our goal.

The components that make up a system are linked together by a relation of interdependence and interaction.

This represents a radical departure from our usual idea of an organization. Interdependence and co-operation among individuals are the opposite of working in perfect isolation, in "closed compartments" regulated by strictly hierarchical relationships, which is how the majority of organizations currently operates.

The closer-knit the interaction among the various components of the system, the greater the need for communication and co-operation among them. Here we will find Deming's diagram useful.

---

* This term comes from Peter Senge's book, *The Fifth Discipline*, Doubleday, 1990.

Bowling Team	Orchestra	Business
Low		High

Degrees of interdependence   (3)

Organizations tend by their very nature to have a high degree of interdependence. Moreover, when a system grows in size and complexity and interacts with external factors (competition, new products, new requirements), it needs to be managed as a set of interacting components.

One of the essential elements of a manager's job is the ability to recognize and manage the interdependencies among the components of the system. This also involves doing everything necessary to satisfy the need for communication among the various components. This has to be achieved by solving conflicts and removing barriers that prevent or complicate the co-operation among individuals and functions.

We have begun to outline the duties and responsibilities of managers who try to manage an organization *systemically*. But let's go back to the definition of a system. It contains a fundamental point that indicates the first action we have to take: *the components of a system work together in order to achieve the goal of the system.*

This is crucial. If there is no goal then there is no system.

So first of all we have to establish the goal of our organization and communicate it to everyone, both internally to the staff of the company, and externally to our suppliers, our customers and our competitors.

Our goal must include plans for the future. We are working from the point of view of continuous improvement, so we need a long-term plan. Management must plan for the future and not be a victim of circumstance.

The kinds of commitment this new attitude brings with it include:

- Continuous learning for all the staff in the organization, regardless of level.
- Constant scanning of the environment the organization interacts with.
- Understanding the need for innovation (product, service and method).

Choosing our goal, deciding how we want to achieve it, and communicating these decisions to everyone means essentially getting our ideas straight and aligning the values of those who work in the organization. In other words, we create a common vision.

When we verbalize this vision we cannot make vague, generalized statements. Indeed, we have to remember that we are providing the basis for the company's strategy and the behavior of our staff at every level.

We must never define a goal purely for methodological purposes. It must always be clear how the goal is going to improve things. The choice of the goal helps make the values of the organization clearer. This means choosing from various possibilities, adopting one direction and excluding another. The end result is a specific and binding commitment. A system has to achieve concrete results.

In addition to the internal organization the goal must be communicated outside the organization. This should include competitors as well as customers.

- Co-operation among competitors to provide the best service to customers is a win-win solution.
- The company must listen to the voice of the customer, but it must also produce innovation and improvement by figuring out the implicit needs the customer does not express.

Our organization has to constantly examine its performance and find out where it can do better, both now and in the future.

The unity and uniformity of purpose in people within the organization is what allows us to create a shared vision; their shared commitment allows our company to focus all its energies on the goal.

If we verbalize the goal of the company bearing all this in mind, then we will also have the ingredients for setting down a long-term management policy that makes sense and achieves consensus.

Deciding on our goal and defining the policies we intend to adopt to achieve it lays the foundation on which we build our organization and establish the values and meaning of our actions. In this way we show that we understand that our organization is a system, and we know which goal we want to focus on.

Measuring the system

In order to steer our system in the right direction we have to know how to make the right decisions. In order to do this it is essential that we be capable of assessing to what extent our system is achieving its goal. In other words, we have to be able to measure the system. In order to do so we need to establish:

- The units the system uses to measure its progress toward the goal.
- A set of measurements suitable for assessing the impact of every local decision on the goal of the system. This in itself forms an adequate support tool for decision-making.

Before we establish in detail the measurements we need, let's clearly focus on the significance of the decisions we must make to manage the system, and the direction we should take.

A manager's job is to coordinate the efforts of all the components of the system in order to achieve the pre-established goal. We call this process *optimizing the system*. Everything that does not optimize the whole system will inevitably lead to losses. Even if we have the best human and technical resources available, if they do not work as a system then our organization will lag behind other companies that may not have our "all star" team but that are managed and operated systemically.

People have to be allowed to interact in such a way that they can see that it is not the sum of their individual efforts but their *coordinated activities* that produce the best results.

Managers have to abandon the idea that the system's performance can be improved by means of the isolated efforts of single functions. For Deming, a leader is a perennial learner, constantly engaged in the improvement of the conditions in which his people interact. In *The New Economics*, Deming points out that managers have to make the best use of people's abilities and inclinations. A group of four people (A,B,C,D) can work in this way:

A+B+C+D (sum of individual abilities)

Or in this way:

(AB)+(AC)+(AD)+(BC)+(BD)+ . . . +(ABC)+(BCD)+

The brackets represent interactions between people in pairs or groups. These interactions can be either positive and helpful, negative and harmful, or zero, producing a net outcome which is bigger or smaller than, or equal to, the individual contributions. As Deming says: "One of management's main responsibilities is to know about the existence of interactions, to perceive how they originate, then to change negative and zero interactions into positive interactions." (4)

In a system, the result achieved by a single individual or function makes sense only in terms of the extent to which it affects the overall result—achieving the goal.

If we continue to use a set of measurements that encourages individuals and single departments to optimize their *local* performances, we undermine the shared vision we established before. It is the strength of this shared vision that increases daily the level of cohesion among people, keeping their actions in line with the common goal.

Now that we have determined the direction our decisions have to go, optimizing overall performance, let's go on to establish the measurements we need.

What measurements do we need?

As organizations can be very different from each other with different kinds of goals, let us try and think of an organization simply as a black box.

How can we measure a black box?

We can measure what we put into the box (the input of the system:I), what the box generates (the output of the system:T), and what we have to spend to make the box work (so that the processes of the system are active:OE). Let's define these three measurements as follows.

- **Inventory—Investment (I):** all the money the system invests to purchase goods.

We say investment to indicate all the money the system gives in exchange for goods that have value. Inventory is also an investment, but could be better defined as the subset of investment that is transformed into Throughput and generates a return for the system. In the manufacturing industry inventory is the raw material purchased. Once it has been processed, raw material is transformed into a finished product and sold. When the client pays for the product, Throughput is generated, the investment produces yield and inventory is reduced. In a school, inventory is represented by the students who have embarked on their studies but who have not yet obtained a diploma.

- **Throughput (T):** the pace with which the system generates units of the goal.

Throughput in for-profit organizations is easy to define: it is the difference between the money that the system obtains from its clients and what it pays to its suppliers to purchase goods and services that are used directly for its products. As far as not-for-profit organizations are concerned, it depends on the goal of the system. For schools, it could be the number of students who obtain a diploma. For hospitals, it could be the number of patients cured, and so on.

- **Operating Expenses (OE):** all the money that the system spends to transform inventory into Throughput.

These measurements fit in well with the intuitive knowledge we have about the system's performance. It is evident that the more we generate Throughput, the closer we get to the goal of our system. It is equally clear that investment and operating expenses should tend toward the minimum amount, as money is a scarce resource. As far as inventory is concerned, it reflects the amount of money invested in raw material that we introduce into our system to generate Throughput. We can also see inventory from another point of view. It in fact reflects the time that passes from the moment we purchase material to the moment the client pays for the finished product. This time is the time necessary to generate Throughput (we can call it Throughput time). This means that, to a certain extent, the shorter the time necessary in order to generate Throughput the lower the inventory.

Intuitively, this looks like good news. If we analyze more closely what a shorter Throughput time means, we will be even more convinced that it will create:

- Improved customer service by supplying closer to 100% of customers' orders on time and within quality expectations [short-term T goes up].
- Lower investment in material, which leads to reduction in operating expenses [OE goes down].
- Potential for additional new orders (that could provide more demand for new products), leading to additional increase in short-term Throughput.
- Potential growth in future Throughput by improving the competitive edge.

So we can see that a reduction in Inventory has a positive impact on the three measurements—T, I and OE. We can therefore conclude that actions to be considered positive for the system are ones that:

- Increase Throughput
- Reduce investments and inventory
- Reduce operating expenses

We need three different measurements because most of the actions taken and decisions made by management have a positive impact on one measurement and a negative impact on another.

Let's look at an example. A manufacturing company in Italy produces automotive components for a big car manufacturer. It is Friday afternoon and an order that is needed for Monday morning in Sweden is not completed yet. The production manager has to make a decision: whether to call people to work on the weekend and use a private airplane to fly the components to the customer, or to carry on with the regular work and ship it late on Tuesday, using their regular method of shipping which is rail and boat. The weekend work and the private plane increase the operating expenses. Concurrently, if they do not ship on time, then immediate Throughput is endangered as the income from the customer will be delayed, they may be subject to a penalty (which reduces income) and their vendor rating will go down, which may jeopardize future orders both from this company and from other companies.

By looking at this problem, we can expect to be in continuous dilemmas about the trade-off between Throughput and operating expenses and inventory/investment. The dilemma springs from the fact that Throughput brings money into the system, whereas investment and operating expenses are taking it out. But there is more to it. There is the issue of timing. The money that is used by OE and I is concurrent. It is here and now, while Throughput lies in the future. This time delay introduces nervousness into the system.

Managers find themselves dealing with a serious conflict. Undoubtedly, in order to make the right decision, they must increase the system's Throughput. To do so they must take action aimed at increasing sales. On the other hand, in order to make the right decision they must reduce the amount of money used by the system, i.e., reduce I and OE.

The sensation is of being in a game you can't win. Whatever decision we make we are bound to lose. The dilemma springs from the simple fact that miracles don't exist. The experience of this dilemma can lead managers to paralysis.

Using the Theory of Constraints to assess decisions

The paralysis is caused by not being able to decide what is better. The solution to this problem is to have a simple, clear-cut mechanism for making these decisions—a way of assessing the impact on our three measurements, T, I and OE. (Throughput, Inventory-Investment and Operating Expense.)

The Theory of Constraints has a simple way of analyzing this and determining whether an action or a decision brings the system closer to its goal or takes it farther away.

In for-profit organizations there are two relevant relationships between the three measurements: T, I, OE.

The difference between Throughput and Operating Expenses

reflects the amount of money left in our hands after deducting the money we pay for operating expenses from the money generated by sales. We must ignore the traditional measurements of cost accounting and consider the difference between T and OE as a close and accurate approximation of the Net Profit.

If the difference between Throughput and Operating Expenses is positive, then the impact of the net profit of the system will be positive, irrespective of the type of financial reporting the system is subject to. This is an important point as, in many cases, managers have difficulty with the connection between their actions and the bottom line results of the company. The only measurements managers should use for decision making are T, I and OE.

Having the simple, practical ability to connect actions to results may upset the financial experts; they may argue that the simplistic definition that the Theory of Constraints gives of net profit is mistaken. The financial definition of the net profit of a system may be more complex, but any system can be considered healthy if Throughput exceeds Operating Expenses. So, we suggest the first assessment mechanism to be:

$$\text{Net Profit (TOC definition)} =$$
$$\text{T (Throughput) minus OE (Operating Expenses)}$$

$$\text{NP (TOC)} = \text{T} - \text{OE}$$

Remember that Throughput already reflects the cost of materials and external services.

The second assessment mechanism is connected to investment. The owners of the organization have invested money in it to pay for the infrastructure and the materials used for generating Throughput. As there is a time delay between money going out to purchase the materials and Throughput money coming in, the shareholders have to finance the working capital.

The providers of the money want to know how well their money is being used. They tend to look at measurements such as ROI (Return On Investment) and ROTA (Return On Total Assets).

Comparing the net profit to the amount of money invested can give us a good indication of the value of the operation for the system's owners. So the second assessment mechanism we propose is:

$$\text{ROI (TOC)} = \frac{\text{Net Profit (TOC)}}{\text{Investment}}$$

which is the same as

$$\frac{\text{Throughput - Operating Expenses}}{\text{Investment}} \quad \text{or} \quad \text{ROI (TOC)} = \frac{\text{T-OE}}{\text{I}}$$

So we have as a set of measurements: T, I, OE, NP (TOC) and ROI (TOC), which together provide good approximations for the financial performance of the organization. This set of measurements can be used by the non-financial managers.

Why measure?

We have to ask ourselves why we need these measurements at all. To answer this question we have to go back and define a manager and his or her role:

- A manager is a person who is responsible for the performance of an area in a system.
- A manager's role is to constantly improve the performance of the area under his or her responsibility.

In order to ensure that the area performs well, the manager has to take actions and make decisions. Without a system of measurement the manager has no guidelines for making good decisions and cannot succeed. A useful measurement is one that provides the bridge between decisions and the bottom line performance of the system. The TOC measurements build that bridge.

When contemplating a decision the manager has to consider the impact it will have on T, I, and OE. The decision will impose an incremental change on one or more of the measurements. Let's call it delta (Δ.)

The proposed action or decision will cause:

ΔT   *change in Throughput*

ΔI   *change in investment*

ΔOE *change in operating expenses*

ΔNP = ΔT − ΔOE is the amount of net money that this decision provides. If the result is positive then the decision makes sense. Therefore a criteria for making a decision can be:

$$\Delta NP = \Delta T - \Delta OE > 0$$

In the case where the decision demands an additional investment, ΔROI can be used to affirm the decision to invest the extra money. ΔROI is the return on investment for the specific investment, and is equal to the ratio of the additional net profit with the additional investment required.

$$\Delta ROI = \frac{\Delta NP}{\Delta I} = \frac{\Delta T - \Delta OE}{\Delta I}$$

The size of ΔROI determines the time it takes to get return on the investment. Top management and the shareholders can make a decision by comparing the proposed investment with other channels for investing money, and satisfying their desire for a proper return on their money.

The Cost Accounting world versus the TOC approach

T, I, OE decision-making seems to be a simple, common sense solution. However, it is a considerable departure from traditional, widely used decision-making processes based on "Cost Accounting." This poses an immediate question.

If cost accounting has been used by so many companies and managers for so long, why should we change to another method?

We need to put this into a historical perspective. Cost Accounting was invented at the beginning of the century. It probably started at Dupont, and continued at General Motors. Cost Accounting was a powerful solution, as there is no doubt that the concept of cost was a major contributor to the huge development of manufacturing in the twentieth century. It provided managers with the ability to make decisions that helped them dramatically improve the performance of their areas and plants. But powerful solutions tend to make themselves obsolete. The stronger a solution the more impact it has on reality, to the extent that the solution *changes* reality and therefore loses its validity.

Some of the basic assumptions of cost accounting became invalid in the 1940s, but as most companies were using the same concepts, the negative impact was not so noticeable. It was only when competition from Asia, especially Japan, became threatening, that people realized there were alternatives. Indeed, the Japanese did not, and still do not, use cost accounting. Those who tried to compete with them using cost accounting methods have been forced into breaking cost rules in order to survive. And decision-making is never so crucial as when companies are struggling to stay alive.

When a measurement system becomes a nightmare

A measurement system should guide people into making good decisions. It becomes a nightmare when it punishes people for doing the right things and promotes and rewards those who do the opposite. Unfortunately, cost-based systems have this danger woven into their fabric.

The problem that cost accounting tries to address is how to make a connection between local actions and decisions and the overall performance of the company. Cost accounting provides this connection by inventing the concepts of product cost and product margin. The assumption behind these ideas is that in order for the company to make money, every single product must be profitable, and the total of profits of the single products is equal to the overall profit. The other assumption is that product cost allows management to get every department and individual to focus on controlling costs.

We can summarize the assumptions of cost systems as:

Product Profit = selling price minus product cost

Company Profit = total of product profits

As long as every product is profitable, the company is safe and sound.

When product margin is a key concept, management focus and actions are aimed at achieving higher margins. Bonuses are given to managers who increase the margins and salespeople who sell products with a higher margin, while low margin products are dumped.

In the mid 1970s and early 1980s managers were faced with severe pressure from Japanese competition, including:

• Reduced prices
• New engineering features
• Better quality

- Better customer service
and the resulting loss of customer loyalty.

As selling prices were dictated by the market and the competitors, companies had to reduce their prices, and so they lost product margins. They were then immediately under pressure to reduce cost.

This is when the cost concept failed to deliver. Managers made decisions that reduced the product cost on paper but not in reality, and cost calculation was directly responsible for many bad decisions. Thousands of jobs were lost.

In order to stay in business companies were not only under pressure to cut costs, they also needed to improve quality and customer service. These improvements were vital to secure future survival, but they demanded investing more money and increasing operating expenses. So the dilemma was: cut costs and save operating expenses, or spend more money on development and improvement?

This is a no-win situation. The limiting factor in this case is a cost-based policy. The major reason is that cost is not suitable for supporting decisions that have no tangible money value attached to them. Unfortunately, all the actions to improve performance come into this category. For example, how do you quantify precisely the impact of improving Due Date Performance from 80% to 95%? Or what will the impact on future sales be of improving product quality from 1000 scrapped parts per million to 50 scrapped parts per million? Cost calculations cannot answer such questions.

Throughout the 1980s and 1990s managers were faced with this dilemma. Cost systems became nightmare measurements. Managers who took actions that improved the competitiveness of the company and had the potential of securing future Throughput were blamed by the cost system and punished by their superiors. Those who went with the flow and complied with the system took actions that were confirmed and praised by their bosses. They reduced costs by re-engineering, laying off workers, squeezing their vendors and cutting corners on quality and service. Actions which were often harmful to individuals and companies.

Too few studies have been conducted and published on companies that went under for us to learn why. Certainly, in our experience, changing the policy of making decisions based on cost accounting can in many cases save companies from misery and misfortune.

Addressing this policy change is not an easy task and may be risky for individual managers in a company. It is dangerous to challenge people from headquarters when one is part of a corporation run on a cost accounting basis.

The solution to this obstacle is to learn the deficiencies of cost-based decisions and learn how to eliminate their negative impact without challenging the people who promote them. The calculations based on T, I and OE can be used in parallel with conventional cost systems. This, however, requires prudence and extra thinking.

At this point we have defined the goal of the system and the operational measurements necessary to guide our organization in the right direction.

STEP TWO
Understanding the system

Let's go back to the definition of a system that we gave earlier: *"a network of interdependent components that work together in order to achieve the goal of the system."*

If we want to reach our goal, we must be sure that the components of our organization behave consistently with respect to the goals we have established. In order to do this we must be capable of thoroughly understanding how these elements in our system interact. This means that we must be able to see our organization as a network of interdependent processes (its components); indeed, we must understand how our system works.

Which tools can supply us with this type of vision? Let's examine the traditional way in which a company is represented by looking at this diagram.

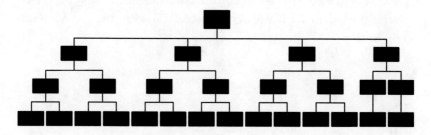

Does this type of hierarchical representation allow us to understand the way our organization works? If we try and understand where the interactions are among the various components, we are unable to come up with a reply. Every company function seems to operate in perfect isolation. The model we use to draw our organization is strictly linked to the way we manage.

The idea which lies at the base of this hierarchical model is that the aim of a company is achieved via the sum of the efforts of single individuals or departments; each one carries out tasks separately and independently from the others, and the total sum of the individual performances is equal to the performance of the company.

In the systemic view however the company goal is achieved thanks to the interaction of individual efforts.

Just think what would happen, for example, if we decided to buy material at the lowest price, or to increase sales, or to spend less on designing or developing products without considering the effects that these kinds of actions might have on the rest of the system and therefore on overall performance.

What we need to concern ourselves with is how to integrate these efforts in order to achieve the goal we have established.

In the hierarchical structure: the "customer" of a particular function is the function above it. The one that controls the work carried out. But in order to see the interaction among the various parts of the system, the customer, who we must absolutely include in the picture, is none other than the component that receives the output of that particular function, what we call the *internal customer*. This interaction is made clear in a diagram Dr. Deming used in all his lessons since 1950—Production Viewed as a System.

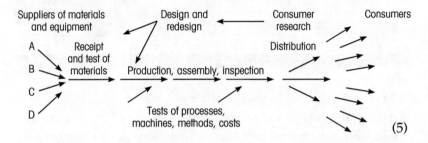

(5)

Another way of making this interaction explicit is the following:

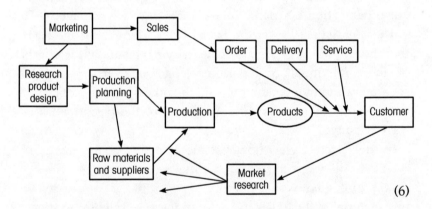

(6)

This way of representing reality shows people what their job is, and indicates how they have to interact with the other components of the system. By looking at this kind of representation, every person in the organization can understand what tasks they have to perform and how they have to cooperate with others. Now we can see the interactions among the various components of the system, including two essential elements that do not appear in the hierarchical diagram: the suppliers and the external customer.

This way of representing the company allows us to go a step deeper and realize that an organization is an open system, in constant interaction with its surrounding environment. This environment, as well as our organization, in turn consists of a series of interdependent processes that are in constant interaction. If we want to understand more about the interactions we must design the main processes that constitute our system.

It is very important for us to have very clear definitions of the concepts we use. So we must define as fully as possible what we mean by process. Let's define a process as a set of steps which, when carried out in a given order, produce a change. Each process is made up of a set of inputs and a set of outputs.

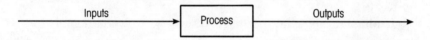

Some of the inputs come from components of the system that actively contribute to the change. Another kind of input is the material itself that the process is acting upon. In other words, what is being changed.

If we want to design the processes in our organization, we have to consult all the people involved. By asking people for their help in this, we are allowing the process to be designed by those who actually do the work—the suppliers of the process (the "active input"), their customers and also those who control the process.

When we design our processes by consulting all those involved, we are able to represent what really happens in our organization, both positive and negative aspects. The representation of the process should tell us:

- Who does what
- What gets done and when
- Which decisions have to be made
- What are the possible consequences of every decision

The simplest and most effective method for designing processes is the deployment flowchart. This tool, which we can use with a reduced set of standard symbols and conventions, provides us with a representation of a sequence of events, activities, steps and decisions that change input in a system or process into output. The deployment flowchart provides us with a wealth of essential knowledge about processes.

- The flow of materials, information and documents
- The various activities which are part of the process
- How the activities change an input into an output
- The interrelations and essential interdependencies between the stages of the process

Understanding these interrelations is a fundamental step toward understanding the systemic nature of our organization. This knowledge is what we need to be able to make the right decisions throughout the process in order to improve it.

The following flowchart (pages 38–39) comes from AISA, a manufacturer of very sophisticated tool machines used for handling glass used in the automotive industry. The flowchart describes the process by which the manufacturer manages requests from clients for spare parts. These spare parts are not actually made by the manufacturer. They could, in fact, be purchased by the machine user directly from the spare parts supplier, thus bypassing the manufacturer. However, clients prefer to pay a higher price and get them from the manufacturer, who is able to guarantee a fast and efficient supply.

The process flow was designed to minimize the time it takes to purchase from the supplier and send the parts to the client. Unfortunately, due to the high level of customization of the machines, the manufacturer cannot always keep the parts in stock and send them immediately. Moreover, as the machines are highly complex, effective purchasing entails close collaboration between the purchasing office, the shipping department and the sales department.

In order to supply products or services to the customer, most processes spill over the boundaries of single functions or offices. They go beyond the hierarchy of the organization chart. When people work together to design the system, knowledge is shared. In this way people are able to see exactly what their contribution is, and how it contributes to achieving the goal of the process.

This in turn fosters continuous improvement. People are able to understand better the best way to do their job. They are not forced to follow procedures laid down by someone who does not really understand the process.

Being able to see how and where the various processes interact allows us to identify internal customers and suppliers. This leads to better relations among the various functions. It also helps us do something Deming considered essential for improvement: break down barriers. The barrier of lack of communication and the barriers between individuals and functions can be overcome. By using a special tool that we will describe later, we can easily and clearly communicate the nature and details of the whole process to everyone involved, even newcomers.

When processes are drawn up as flowcharts and compared with the ideal way they should be carried out in order to be consistent with our organization's goal, we can spot various negative aspects.

For example, we will find unnecessary complications in the flow; these may arise from temporary solutions adopted to cope with an unexpected difficulty, but which have then become standard practice. In this case we have to identify the activities which do not add any value to the process, but which have become "routine" since they were installed to solve a particular problem.

In other cases complications in the process may be the result of a hierarchical management style—too much control of the system interrupts the flow of operations with constant "loops" of action. We need only think of those processes where people's activities are constantly blocked by the need for authorization

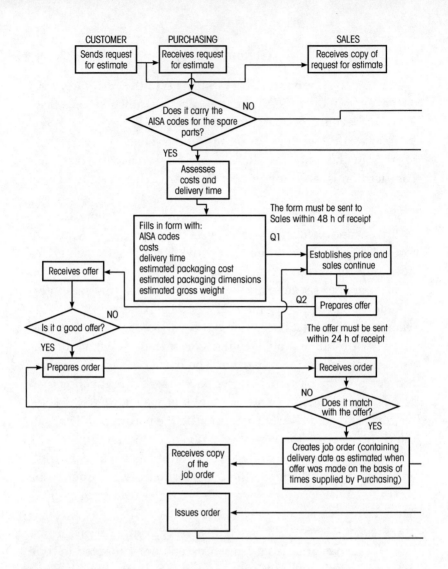

CUSTOMER PURCHASING SALES

Sends request for estimate

Receives request for estimate

Receives copy of request for estimate

Does it carry the AISA codes for the spare parts? NO

YES

Assesses costs and delivery time

The form must be sent to Sales within 48 h of receipt

Q1

Fills in form with:
AISA codes
costs
delivery time
estimated packaging cost
estimated packaging dimensions
estimated gross weight

Establishes price and sales continue

Receives offer

Q2

Prepares offer

The offer must be sent within 24 h of receipt

Is it a good offer? NO

YES

Prepares order

Receives order

NO

Does it match with the offer?

YES

Receives copy of the job order

Creates job order (containing delivery date as estimated when offer was made on the basis of times supplied by Purchasing)

Issues order

TECHNICAL OFFICE	SHIPPING DEPARTMENT	ADMINISTRATION	SUPPLIERS

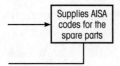

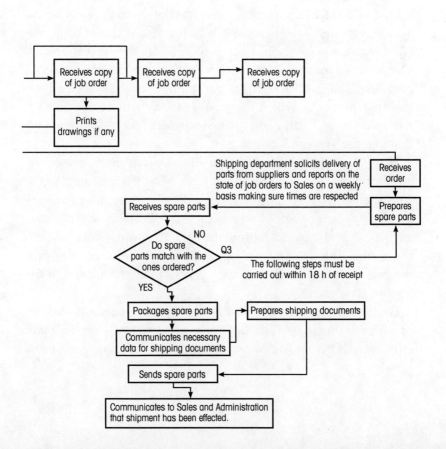

from superiors. In yet other instances there are points between one process and another where there is an actual interruption between internal suppliers and internal customers.

Flowcharts are useful for identifying "Key Quality Characteristics." Those characteristics are aspects of the processes that endanger the capacity to achieve the goal. They are identified above all on the basis of two criteria: they are closely linked with the customer-supplier relationship, and they are at points in the flow where a (Yes, No) choice is required. As we will see in Step Three, the Key Quality Characteristics help us gather data about the process so we can monitor the stability and performance of the system in different phases, as well as verify the effectiveness of action taken to improve the system itself. The advantage we gain from these indicators is an ever-increasing focus on the customer and, as we will see in Step Three, the elimination of excessive variation.

In all these cases, when we examine the process we have designed and we find inconsistencies in relation to the goal of the system, we then have to redesign the process so that it conforms with that goal. We should never forget that the system and its components constantly interact with the surrounding environment and that reality changes constantly. So it may often happen that processes which make sense today will be obsolete tomorrow. If we carry on using obsolete processes we will damage the system.

Using flowcharts allows us to identify which processes, or parts of them, are superfluous or have lost their meaning in the face of changes within the system and the surrounding environment. If these are not checked, they can become consolidated with time and lead to logical "snags" in the network of processes. For this reason it is up to those who manage the processes to intervene with prompt updates in conformity with the goal of the system.

People within the organization learn from processes. Everyone is encouraged to describe the way they actually do their job. However, if we really want this to happen, managers must adopt a set of measurements and a new reward system which focuses their actions, and consequently everyone else's, on the overall result of the system. As we saw previously, if we continue to use an approach that measures and assesses results locally, as with traditional cost accounting, then it is impossible to optimize the overall results of the organization.

Managers themselves will also have considerable difficulty in taking into consideration the measurement of processes if they continue to be judged on the output they produce. This is why one of the later steps in our Decalogue—Step Seven—deals explicitly with creating the right sort of management structure. In Step Seven we will examine the logic and the framework this structure has to be built upon, and we will clarify the reasons why this has to be dealt with at a relatively late stage of our transformation process.

When managers try to redesign the system and redefine the company processes so they are in line with the goal, they will meet with resistance from the people in the organization who work on those processes. Not everyone will have the same perception of the goal of the system, in some cases there will be disagreement about the nature of the problem in question and the direction that should be taken.

In other cases, as people tend to focus on local optimization, they will react badly to interference with "their" process, and will feel personally threatened and less secure.

Two fundamental points from Deming's doctrine are:

- Drive out fear
- Break down barriers

If managers want to implement solutions that bring about effective change, they have to be able to deal with the fear and conflicts which get in the way. People's levels of resistance to change, as we will see in more depth later on, take on various forms according to the degree of awareness and participation the solution requires of them. Eli Goldratt's Thinking Processes tools help us overcome these levels of resistance.

The tool that helps us solve the conflicts that can arise in the phase of designing and redesigning processes is called a *conflict cloud*. The conflict cloud increases people's ability to construct and communicate win-win solutions. This helps overcome people's tendency to solve conflicts by means of compromises that can often bring about lose-lose situations. We use this tool in a negotiation situation where there is no acceptable compromise. We verbalize our position and that of our counterpart. We then go on to identify the needs which the opposing positions are trying to satisfy. Finally, we look for the common goal, the reason which drives both parties to seek a solution which is acceptable for all.

In this way we move from a situation of "you against me because of the problem" to "you and me against the problem."

The solution to the conflict is provided by an "injection" that separates the need from the conflicting position. In this way it invalidates an assumption which connects the position taken by one of the sides to the need they are trying to satisfy. An example of a conflict cloud, as well as other Thinking Processes Tools, are given in Chapter 5.

To deal with the negative reservations people may have about the solutions and changes to the processes proposed, the Thinking Process tool we can use is called NBR—Negative Branch Reservation. This tool allows us to map out in detail the logic of our thought process when we think a proposed solution will lead to a negative effect. In order to build this picture we list all the negative effects we think will be the result of implementing the proposed solution. We then connect the proposed solution with the negative effects we suspect will derive from it, by means of cause-effect relations.

At this point, when we present the logic of the negative branch, we reveal some hidden assumptions that lead people to respond negatively to change. All the assumptions on the NBR can be subjected to a challenge that negates them with injections. These injections can help us remove the NBR.

Dealing properly with negative response is necessary for three main reasons:

- To protect and immunize the proposed changes from unexpected difficulties.
- To get the buy-in of the people who tend to be devil's advocates.
- To demonstrate leadership through listening and incorporating relevant input.

At the end of this second step we have obtained an essential result for our transformation process. We have designed and redefined the processes of our system so that they are consistent with the goal of the system. When we design and examine processes we provide ourselves with fundamental elements which allow us to manage change.

Moreover, having a clear and constant vision of the system allows us to clearly see the implications our actions and decisions have for processes. This allows us to study the results and decide how to behave. In other words, we have a tool for improving the system.

STEP THREE
Making the system stable

In the previous step we designed the processes that make up our organizations in a way that is in line with the goal. By doing this we get a clear vision of the processes of our system and how they interact.

We can understand what the implications of our actions and decisions are for processes, and therefore for the system as a whole. This means we have created the conditions for improving the system.

But in order to improve the system we must be able to answer further questions. What influences the system's behavior and as the system is made up of a network of interdependent processes, how do those processes behave? In what way can the behavior of a process influence the behavior of the system? In operational terms, what are the consequences of the answers to these questions, i.e., what actions should we undertake?

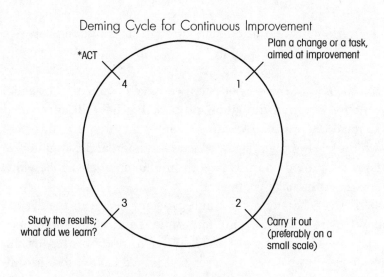

Deming Cycle for Continuous Improvement

Plan a change or a task, aimed at improvement

*ACT

4

1

3

2

Study the results; what did we learn?

Carry it out (preferably on a small scale)

*ACT	Adopt the change.
or	Abandon it.
or	Run through the cycle again, possibly under different environmental conditions.

(7)

Our system interacts with the surrounding environment, which changes continuously. Likewise, the improvement process we apply to the system must itself be continuous. What is continuous improvement? Understanding the nature and meaning of this process means getting to the heart of a manager's job.

Deming described the ability to predict as fundamental. When we are able to understand the impact of our actions on the entire system, then we can anticipate the development of events and have more control over them. The ability to predict is therefore the essence of management. Indeed it is the essential requirement for managing a system. But it is difficult for us to predict because systems, by their very nature, tend to be unstable, i.e., to produce unpredictable results.

Stability is not normal behavior for a system; it is instead an objective that we have to reach. So, if we want to have control over our actions, we must make sure the system we act upon is stable. In other words, it must produce predictable results.

If we take action to improve the stability of a system without knowing if it is in statistical control, we can destroy the system itself. Therefore, the first thing we must do is measure the system's stability or lack of it.

Control charts and reducing variation

Control charts were a tool devised to measure and improve the variability of a system. They were developed by Walter Shewhart in the 1920s as a result of his work at Bell Laboratories. The control chart offers a much fuller picture than commonly used comparison of data to specifications or to average values of performance. These measurements will only tell us if performance is in or out of specs, above or below average. They tell us nothing about the process which produces these values.

At first glance, a control chart resembles a time series graph. In a time series graph, monthly sales for example, we plot months of the year along the horizontal axis, and the number of products sold along the vertical axis. However, as a time series graph only makes comparisons between single values it does not give us sufficient information about the behavior of a process, whether it is in or out of control, predictable or not.

The control chart, which in every respect is a process behavior chart, instead puts this information into a context by adding three horizontal lines. The central line acts as a reference against which we identify trends. The other two lines are control limits—the upper and lower control limits, or natural process limits.*

In the following diagram, we can see a control chart of a stable process. It contains data regarding the percentage of shipments made within the time forecast by a manufacturing company.

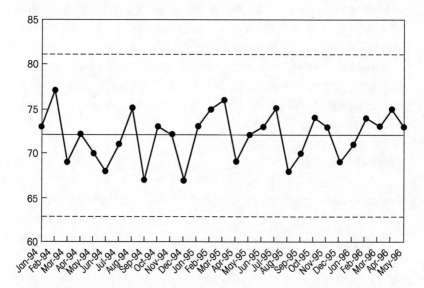

This chart shows a process which is likely to be in control because none of the points of the chart is higher above the upper control limit nor below the lower control limit. The importance of this graph is that, unless major changes occur in the execution of the shipment process, next month's shipments will be, approximately, between 63% and 81% within time forecast.

---

* These are calculated with the help of coefficients using the average values from a time series graph and moving ranges, i.e., the differences between the individual values of the time series. They are based on the concept of "3 sigma," sigma being a measure of the spread of data around an average value. For further information on 3 sigma and control charts in general see Don Wheeler's excellent explanations in *Understanding Statistical Process Control*, SPC Press, 1992.

Let's look at the chart related to a process that is *not* in statistical control. Inventory of work-in-process of the same company we looked at before.

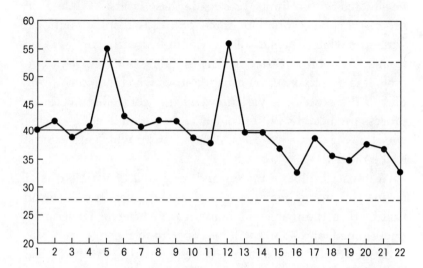

This second diagram shows a process that is out of control. In fact two points lie above the upper control limit, and more than eight consecutive points are below the average-central line.* A process which is so out of control has a future behavior that is unpredictable.

Control charts are the tools that enable us to take meaningful actions. Depending on whether a process is in control or not, the action we take will differ radically. It is the manager's job to understand the kind of variation in the processes in order to take the appropriate actions to improve them.

We can use a flowchart to measure and improve the stability of our system, its predictability, by applying control charts to the main processes of our system which we have shown on the flowchart. Indeed, as our flowcharts allow us to see all the stages of the process clearly, they help us to identify the best

---

* The rules for detection of out of control processes can be found in Wheeler, *Understanding Statistical Process Control*.

points for gathering data in order to build our control charts, and thus calculate the variation of the processes.

According to Shewhart, the variation of a process could either be situated within limits, or outside these limits: "While every process displays variation, some processes display controlled variation, while others display uncontrolled variation." (8) Controlled variation is variation that is stable and consistent over time. It is due to common causes, causes which are intrinsically part of the process. A variation which is controlled makes the process predictable. But uncontrolled variation is not consistent over time. It is due to special causes, causes which are external to the process.

We must absolutely understand *what kind* of variation is affecting the process we are examining. If the variation is uncontrolled, then the manager's ability to predict will be seriously undermined, and so too will his capacity to manage.

In Shewhart's words, "A phenomenon will be said to be controlled when, through the use of past experience, we can predict, at least within limits, how the phenomenon may be expected to vary in the future." (9)

Failing to identify the source of variation, special or common, leads to taking inappropriate actions on the system that may worsen the situation. Deming called that tampering with the system.

As Brian Joiner points out in his book, *Fourth Generation Management*, in order to improve an out-of-control process we must:

1. Gather data immediately so that the *special causes* which generate the instability of the system are quickly identified.
2. Activate an immediate solution to limit the damage.
3. Look for what has determined the occurrence of the *special cause*.
4. Implement a long-term solution.

In order to improve a process that is in control, we have various options for acting on it. We can:

1. Stratify the data, dividing it into categories based on various factors, and analyze how the points of data are or are not grouped together.
2. Separate the data, dividing it into various components and dealing with them separately.
3. Experiment by applying the continuous improvement cycle (which we saw at the beginning of Step Three); carry out planned experiments and learn from the effects observed.

We achieve Quality and the continuous improvement of the system's processes by constantly reducing the sources of variation that undermine the predictability of the processes. Predictability can only be obtained by incessantly pursuing the uniformity, consistency and reliability of our processes.

Let's recap the results we have achieved so far.

1. The data we need to analyze the system and support decision-making must be presented in a suitable way.
2. The first problem to face in order to construct continuous improvement in our organizations is to understand the kind of variation which is affecting our processes.
3. The actions we take to improve our processes differ radically depending on the nature of the variation that affects them.

But what usually happens in our organizations? Normally, we don't think about processes. We just act in order to satisfy specifications.

There is confusion in the marketplace between product specifications and controlled processes. The product specifications are the measurements imposed by the customer in order to declare when products or services will be acceptable to them and fit for their purposes. As we have seen, a process is said to be in control when the pattern of its variability is predictable within limits. The respect for specifications and the predictability of processes in principle have nothing in common.

Let's look at the problem more closely: reducing the variation of a process means making the results we get from it more consistent and reliable, i.e, more predictable. If we focus on satisfying specs, we lose sight of the problem of reducing variation. By limiting our efforts to satisfying specs we do not allow ourselves to understand the reliability and repeatability of our processes. Without this understanding we will not be able to guarantee our customers in the future the excellent results we are getting now. This is because we don't understand how the process that generates those results behaves. The power of Walter Shewhart's approach to understanding variation lies in allowing us to understand if the results obtained by our process are consistent, repeatable and reliable, in other words predictable. (Shewhart was Deming's teacher.)

To further clarify the relation between the specification's approach and Shewhart's approach, let's examine the kind of states a process can find itself in. The following classifications come from Don Wheeler's, *Understanding Statistical Process Control*.

The ideal state

In this state the process is in statistical control and produces 100% of conforming products. What are the characteristics of a process in this state? What do we have to do to achieve it?

- The process must be stable over time.
- The natural spread of the process must be inferior to the tolerance specified for the product.
- We must act on the process in a stable and consistent way.

- Conditions cannot be changed arbitrarily.
- The average of the process must be set and maintained.

The threshold state

In this state the process will display a reasonable degree of statistical control, but it will produce some non-conforming products; the fact that the process is in control means that the number of non-conforming products will remain more or less regular over time. The only two ways to guarantee 100% of conforming products in this case are to:

- Change the specifications
- *Act on the process to reduce the variation*

The brink of chaos state

In this state the process is out of control even though it is producing 100% of conforming products. This is a particular situation. Indeed, everything seems to be going fine, but the process is affected by special causes of variation that undermine the stability of the process and make its development unpredictable.

In other words, a process of this type can degenerate any moment, thus altering the quality and conformity of its output.

Chaos

Here the process is both out of statistical control and produces non-conforming products. It's impossible to determine the percentage of non-conformity produced by this process over time. The only way to come out of this state of chaos is to first remove the special causes of variation.

As can be seen, we can give the customer 100% of what he wants operating a process which is unstable. Conversely we can consistently produce something out of specs while operating in a predictable manner.

Which is the best? In general, we can't say. What we can say is that a state of control is not a natural state for a process and entropy *does* exist. In other words, a process that presently has an outcome that satisfies the customer, but is highly unstable, is very likely to degenerate into a chaotic state without much warning. This is the risk that we run if we operate our processes in a state which is on the brink of chaos.

Angelo Panozzi is the president of a relatively small, but well-known, printing company in the north of Italy. He keeps running records on many of the company's performances. He is particularly proud of last month's on-time delivery rate—over 95%. Here's how he might talk to his secretary.

"Look at this! This is terrific!" Angelo remarked. The running record showed an impressive series of percentages. "No one can compete with us," Angelo triumphantly summarized for Carla, his secretary.

Carla stared for a second at the running chart.

"I guess we might look at these figures the way Stefano suggested the other day. . . ."

"Ah, Stefano," was Angelo's reaction, "he is such a lovely kid! He is doing a great job with the people on the shop floor, they love him . . . Did he say something about the on-time delivery rate?"

"Yes," was Carla's hesitant answer. "I thought he would comment on that in a different way."

"What do you mean?" Angelo asked.

"You know," Carla kept on, "he always comes up with these ideas. He says that we should, I mean . . . we should try not to limit our analysis to the running chart."

"But the results speak for themselves," was Angelo's proud reaction. "This time, I think Stefano is wrong."

Carla did not say anything, but the historical on-time delivery rates that she computed gave the following picture.

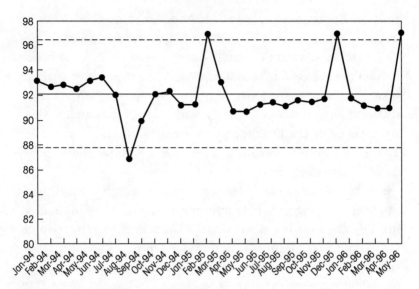

This process is said to be out of control. As a matter of fact, we couldn't even call it a process; it portrays a series of loosely connected events.

How could we comment on the delivery performance Mr. Panozzi seems so happy about? It is a very impressive series of positive results with no degree whatsoever of repeatability.

What Panozzi's company has delivered in the past has no guarantee of being repeated in the future. His company's performance is not predictable. Remember, the essence of management, any form of management, is prediction. If we cannot predict the outcome of a performance, we cannot manage it. Should we then be unhappy with such a performance?

The real question is: what is preventing Panozzi from achieving better stability in his performance? And, how much is this unpredictability costing him? These are, in fact, the two main reasons for not wanting out-of-control processes. The first one is connected with the impossibility of predicting, which often translates into the impossibility of planning, making programs or schedules, or meeting customer specs. The second one is connected with the cost associated with running such a messed-up process. In fact, performances that appear to be good often disguise a very poor optimization in the use of resources.

Control charts are the way to detect the effect that our actions had on the system. If the assumptions were right and the actions taken properly carried out, the process will oscillate around a different average value, possibly with a lower variability. This is the essence of the Deming Cycle for continuous improvement. This is the only way to act rationally to achieve the improvement of a performance.

For Walter Shewhart, Deming's great teacher, Quality is defined as "On target with minimum variance." Throughout his life Dr. Deming led a passionate campaign to raise people's awareness of the danger of not understanding the nature of variability. In order to achieve this understanding Deming promoted vigorously the use of Statistical Process Control (SPC) and control charts. When asked to define the role of management today, how many people would mention SPC?

Reducing variation was the essence of management for Deming. It is the lack of this awareness which accounts for much of the failure in contemporary management practice. Budgeting and budgeting techniques are examples of a management approach governed by conformance to specifications. They are based on estimates that are often arbitrary. These estimates almost invariably translate into equally arbitrary targets. The achievement of these targets, or failure to do so, becomes the basis for managerial decisions. These decisions shape the way in which people relate to the organization, the way they work and, ultimately, the way they are in the world.

Budgets, like specs in production, are "the voice of the customer." They represent what we would like to achieve, or what the customer is asking us to deliver. Neither of the two has anything to do with what we can achieve or deliver.

According to Deming, the role of a leader is to create the environment that allows people to take joy in their work, use their abilities and fulfill their potential. In order to do that the leader must eliminate fear in the workplace. As Dr. Deming points out there are two circumstances to consider.*

1. The worker has achieved statistical control of his/her work.
2. The worker has not yet achieved statistical control of his/her work. (10)

Again, the two states will call for a different set of actions, none of which entails blaming the worker. We must remember that poor performances are very often due to lack of understanding of the system that people operate in and, in many cases, the answer is in training.

Deming's work represents the most fundamental contribution to achieving Quality. The goal of his work is to acquire profound knowledge of the impact that actions have on a system. This approach encourages the study of effects in order to search for the root causes which determined them. Consequently the focus of attention opens up from the narrow realm of emphasizing results to the wider possibilities of examining processes. This is the key to achieving greater control over our actions and increasing our chances of predicting their outcome.

In Deming's approach, the ability to predict is the very essence of management. What more than anything else blocks our ability to predict? As we have seen, it is variation.

Maximum Quality is the result of minimum variation in processes. The processes which make up a system or organization are interdependent. If we do not understand the variation of processes, we cannot know what impact our efforts might have on improving a performance elsewhere. For these reasons the goal of Step Three is to achieve a stable system.

In his constant search for Quality, Deming created a complex and rigorous theory. Applying this theory requires considerable

* Chapter eight of *Out of Crisis* contains the foundation for redefining the work of resource managers.

determination and intellectual commitment on our part. In order for this extraordinary theory to yield the benefits we hope for, we need effective tools that can interpret and translate this complexity into something we can use on a practical level. The Theory of Constraints offers these tools.

TOC enables us to interpret situations by analyzing the cause-effect relationships that make up our reality. This analysis is made possible by means of logical tools called the Thinking Processes (TP). The Thinking Processes help us overcome difficult obstacles in the process of change involved in all continuous improvement.

When we use the tools we are able to answer logically and systematically the three questions at the heart of any process of change. What to change? What to change to? How to make the change possible?

The Thinking Processes are based on a logic of necessity and sufficiency. In many cases this logic allows us to highlight the kind of cause-effect relationship governing the situations we are examining. The tools guide us in investigating and visually representing the logical connections which exist within organizations and which determine the way they work.

In this sense we can say that the TOC tools are in line with Deming's approach and constitute a valid means of bringing about the implementations of his ideas.

Achieving stability, the goal of Step Three, enables us to think about how to improve the system's performance and increase its Throughput. Our aim is to find a way to get the maximum result from a stable system.

The TOC approach shifts management efforts to achieving the goal through focusing on the factor which limits the system's performance—the constraint.

This is done by means of the Five Focusing Steps. They allow us to identify and manage the constraint. This focusing is made possible with the help of the Thinking Processes which takes a concrete shape in its applications to the various areas of an organization (Drum-Buffer-Rope for production, Critical Chain for project management).

Therefore the goal of the next step will be to identify the constraint and carry out the Five Focusing Steps.

Chapter 2

Managing Systems Through Constraints

Steps 4, 5, 6

The weakest link in a chain is the strongest because it can break it.

STANISLAW J. LEC (11)

A wise man is strong; yea, a man of knowledge increaseth strength.

MISHLEI (BOOK OF PROVERBS) 24:5

STEP FOUR
Identify the constraint and carry out the Five Focusing Steps

Let's go back to looking closely at our organization. As we have seen in Step One and in more in detail in Step Two, we can easily perceive our system as a set of various components that interact with each other. We called these components interdependent processes. We saw that these processes have to be designed so that they are consistent with their common goal—the goal of the system. We have understood the concept of variation and the need for process stability. How should we design our system and make it work in order to obtain the maximum results from it?

Let's try to imagine how a very simple system behaves, where every step corresponds to an operation which, in a production process, feeds the following step. Our instinctive wish, not only ours but of anyone who has ever managed, is to balance the system. Our ideal is probably a system built like a perfectly straight tube with the same diameter all along it. In such a system everything that goes in must come out. But does it really happen like this? A simple experiment shows a very different reality.

If we build such a system, where the average value of production equals the demand, every step determines the Throughput of the system. Let's try and see what happens if we begin to make such a system work by doing a trial production cycle. In cycle one, the first step will pass on to the second step anything from 6 to 14 units, say 13. The second step will perform from 6 to 14 units, say 10. The third one from 6 to 14, say 10. The fourth one from 6 to 14, say 11. And the fifth one from 6 to 14, say 7. What is the result at the end of cycle one?

Step one will deliver 13 units to step two. Step two will be able to work only on 10 of these units. Step three will receive the 10 units, work all of them and pass them all to step four. Step four could handle 11, but it only has 10, so it will pass the 10 to step five. Step five has capacity only for 7, so 3 will stay behind and 7 will be the final Throughput of the first cycle.

In summary, 13 went in and 7 came out. And what about the other 6? Three are locked between steps one and two and the other three between steps four and five.

The first thing we observe is that, as the various steps are linked together and dependent on each other, we always find that a part of the material which is released at the beginning produces work in progress along the process. This prevents us from satisfying the demand in time.

The second cycle will certainly provide different performance indicators as the different steps are working to different values (within the expected variation) and the available work in progress is captured between the steps.

What happens? With the passing of time, the accumulation of work in progress uncouples the steps and they can operate independently from each other. At this point, idle time between steps disappears and the Throughput of the process increases to the average capacity of the balanced steps.

Does this kind of solution allow us to achieve our goal? It does not for the following two reasons.

1. Until the work in progress unlocks the dependent steps, our system will always deliver less than the stated average capacity of the individual steps. Moreover, the amount of time needed for the unlocking is heavily influenced by the range of variation of the individual steps.

2. This cycle has to be repeated for every product change. If these changes are frequent, there will never be enough time to reach the state where the steps are uncoupled and the Throughput of the system will never be as large as the average capacity of the steps.

The cause of our problems is the excessive variability of the processes. We know how to behave in these cases: we have to discover the root cause of this variability, because only once we have identified it can we develop a sufficiently complete solution.

Let's go back to our previous example:

If the average capacity of all the steps but one is increased, so that the whole system has only one bottleneck, i.e., a resource that doesn't have enough capacity to produce the load imposed on it (we call it the *constraint*), and we manage the workflow according to the constraint, and the demand is equal to (or less than) the average production rate of the constraint, then we can meet schedule (provided that the variation around the average value for the production rate of the constraint and the variation in demand are not too high).

The Five Focusing Steps are the model developed by Goldratt for managing systems. Here they are in a condensed form:

Focusing Step 1: Identify the constraint(s) of the system

Generally we can identify a constraint in a system on the basis of the interval of variability of its processes, and by observing how they interact. Indeed, we assume these intervals of variability to show stability (to be in control); if they do not, each of them sooner or later will become a constraint.

Naturally, depending on the environment we find ourselves in, the constraint will be different. In a production environment the constraint is likely to be the production stage where work in progress is generated.

If, instead, we wish to apply this solution to project environments, we must identify the Critical Chain, which is the longest succession of dependent events that determines the length of the whole project, where the dependence of the events is not only due to a temporal relation but also to the fact that the same resource is used for more than one activity. As the constraint is what limits our Throughput, we must move to the next step.

Focusing Step 2: Decide how to exploit the constraint of the system

Exploit is the right word. We have no other choice. As the constraint is what limits the system's Throughput, we have to make it work to the maximum. As we have decided how to manage the constraint, we must ask ourselves the same question about all the other components of the system. This brings us to the next Focusing Step.

Focusing Step 3: Subordinate everything else to the decision taken regarding the constraint

All the other components of the system must work so that they guarantee the full-speed functioning of the constraint. The rest of the system is subordinated to the activity of the constraint.

Once we have gotten this far, the constraint is producing to the maximum. What can we do to further increase Throughput?

Focusing Step 4: Elevate the constraint

We can increase the capacity of the constraint. It is the only thing left for us to do. Depending on the nature of the constraint, we add a machine, or resources. At this point, if our constraint is no longer the constraint, we go to Focusing Step 5.

Focusing Step 5: Go back to Focusing Step 1

A new constraint will take over from the previous one and we have to start the cycle all over (but without allowing inertia to generate a new constraint).

Before we apply this management model to our organization, let's look at our system again a bit more closely. We said that the system has a goal to achieve. Throughput is the measurement of how much the goal is being achieved.

Our aim is to ever increase Throughput. How does our organization generate Throughput? Throughput is achieved by means of the interaction of many resources and disciplines in the organization. This is known as the Throughput chain. What is the Throughput chain?

It is a chain of dependent efforts of different people, departments or organizations. It is also known as the supply chain. For example, in a manufacturing organization Throughput is achieved only when the cash collected from the customer arrives safely in the company's bank account. Before that happens many people have to contribute their efforts. Someone has to design the product, others have to market it, sell it, purchase raw materials, produce, test, ship, invoice and collect the money. Usually, these people work in different departments.

Managing the Throughput Chain

The T-chain is itself a system and therefore it has its own constraint. Theoretically, there should be only one constraint in the chain. However, in reality we find the paradoxical situation in which two or more constraints interact within the same chain. For example, a company may have a lack of customer orders, and yet when an order arrives, it is shipped late as if there was a capacity constraint.

Managing the Throughput chain means that, given the stability of all the links, the first thing we must do within any system is identify which is the weakest link, and then take the link through Goldratt's Five Focusing Steps.

As there are different links in the chain, there are also different applications of the Five Focusing Steps for these links. Some of the applications are more generic and some less. Traditionally the Goldratt ideas are associated with Production and Logistics, but over the years the way of improving systems (we call it the knowledge tree—we will discuss this later) has been proven to generate a remarkable body of knowledge in other links as well.

Theory of Constraints (TOC) Applications currently available to address constraints in different links are:

- DBR—Drum Buffer Rope for Production and Logistics Management
- Distribution—for supply chain management

- Critical Chain—for project management and product development
- "Unrefusable Offer"—marketing and sales

There are hundreds more applications that were constructed by individual representatives from organizations. They deal with links and situations that are specific to their reality. Next, we will describe the application for managing systems the TOC way, for Production and Logistics, known as DBR and for Project Management, known as Critical Chain.

When we deal with steps Eight and Nine in our Decalogue, we will illustrate the application for marketing and sales.

Production Management using TOC

Drum Buffer Rope (DBR) and Buffer Management (BM)

Production using TOC means applying the Five Focusing Steps for managing the production and logistic links on the Throughput chain.

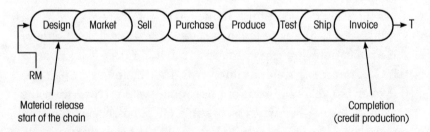

Design) Market) Sell) Purchase) Produce) Test) Ship) Invoice → T

RM

Material release
start of the chain

Completion
(credit production)

Production and logistics systems are about moving material through a series of synchronized activities performed by different resources. The role of production and logistics is to produce finished products that are turned into Throughput when the customer receiving the goods is satisfied with the content and the service provided.

Most production processes are more complex than the one presented here, but we will use this simplified version to demonstrate the logic of the solution and the thinking behind it.

We use the terms *production* and *logistics* together, as in some organizations the role of moving the material may be split between two different lines of responsibilities. Ensuring that the operator produces the right part within specs and quality is the role of the production manager, whereas the role of instructing people on which job to work and when—loading the machine—may be in the hands of production control as a part of material management (logistics).

Overview

Improving systems. What do we mean by improving the production system?

There are two major indicators that the production and logistics links are a constraint of the entire T-chain.

1. Due Date Performance (DDP) is not good. Less than 100% on-time delivery, is unaccepted by the customers. (DDP can be in the high nineties, but customers may still complain and threaten to take their business elsewhere.)
2. Manufacturing Lead Time is too long. The time from the start of the production to the time the product is ready to be shipped to the customer is too long, making it difficult to keep existing customers and gain new orders.

The first situation means that the production and logistics performance constrains the current Throughput, whereas long lead time constrains future Throughput. In the case where current Throughput is jeopardized, there is a need to take immediate action to get control and ensure 100% DDP, or it may endanger the long-term stability of the system.

Using the Focusing Steps

What is the constraint of the system?

When DDP is less than 100% the constraint is anything that blocks the flow on its journey from material release to the customer. It can be a bottleneck—a resource that doesn't have enough capacity to produce the load imposed on it; it can be a resource that has capacity fluctuations due to uncontrolled load or machine breakdown.

The most visible disruption to the flow is a resource that causes a capacity constraint that is called CCR—Capacity Constraint Resource.

If it is not a capacity constraint, then it is either an out of control resource or an out of control process.

When Lead Time (LT) is too long, the constraint is everything that prevents the system from reducing the lead time. When investigating the reasons, we will find that they are the same as before.

- CCR (Capacity Constraint Resource)
- Out of control resource
- Out of control process

Managers and production people should be given the tools to identify the constraints to the flow, and be encouraged to use process improvement methods to get the resources and processes under control.

How do we know we have a problem in the production area?

Throughput is the number one issue! This means that the only way the company can generate money is through producing and shipping customers' orders. This means that in both cases (DDP less than 100% and LT too long) the real constraint of the entire system is customer orders. Therefore, Focusing Step 1 states: The constraint is customers' orders.

Please note that in some companies production is remote from the market and products are shipped to a distribution center. In this case the stock orders, or replenishment orders, should be treated as the constraint—the company is paid when delivering the goods on time to the next link in the internal supply chain.

Decide how to exploit the system constraint

Exploiting means making the most of the little we have—squeezing the maximum. What is the meaning of exploiting the "Production Orders"? It simply means not wasting the little that we have. Even if we have many orders, we still need more in order to increase overall performance. It means shipping everything in time and within specification and within budget.

Time is a major element in generating Throughput. When we deliver in conformity within the time the customer wants the goods, we get paid. Therefore, we make the most of the customers' orders *when we deliver on time*. Therefore, the decision regarding how to exploit the system constraint is to have a detailed plan for shipping the goods—*a shipping schedule.*

So, when we have a shipping schedule, we have a detailed plan of when the orders have to be ready. When we focus our actions on meeting the shipping schedule, we ship the orders on time and generate the maximum Throughput we can (given the current order book). This is what is meant by exploiting. The plan for exploiting the constraint is known as the "DRUM." This term was used when the solution was developed by Dr. Goldratt. He used the analogy of marching soldiers or Boy Scouts on a day trip (as presented in Goldratt's books *The Goal, The Race* and *The Haystack Syndrome).*

A secondary drum

In the rare case that a production area experiences a bottleneck, or a severe CCR, there may be a high risk that the shipping schedule is not realistic. In this case there will be a need to introduce a *secondary drum*—a plan to exploit the capacity constraint.

The Secondary Drum will regulate the use of the Capacity Constraint Resource to exploit the Capacity Constraint. This will be in terms of a detailed schedule that will determine what the CCR is expected to perform—a sequence of jobs needed to support the shipping schedule.

It is possible that the secondary drum will create delays that cause delays in the order completions, and hence inability to ship on time. In this case, actions must be taken to cope with the situation, such as informing the customers about potential delays or finding ways to temporarily increase the available capacity.

Subordinate everything else to the above decision

Managing the T-chain suggests that, once identified, managers must focus on their system's constraint(s). However, there are many other things that managers are supposed to take care of. There are all the resources. Even if there are a few that are CCRs, the majority are not. What do we do with them? How do we manage them? We can't let them go loose as this will lead to chaos.

Focusing Step 3 gives us the answer. Control the work released to the shop floor. The more material that is kept in the WIP (Work In Progress) area, the greater the degree of freedom the operators have and the more need there is for management and production control interference to ensure that the right parts are worked on. This is known as expediting.

The first part of subordination is called *Rope*. It means controlling the material released to the pace consumed by the drum.

When to release the material is determined by the length of time needed to allow the journey from material release to the drum. This is called *Buffer Time* and it is the third element in the approach hereafter known as *Drum-Buffer-Rope*.

Drum-Buffer-Rope is only a part of the change. It reflects the change in the way we plan production. But there is something else we have to consider. How do we handle the reality we face when the plan is released? Everybody knows what the lifetime of a production plan is. In many cases the plan is already invalid before the ink has a chance to dry.

How can we guarantee the on-time arrival of the right goods to the shipping dock? What if:

- Operators do not subordinate to the schedule?
- There are Capacity Constrained Resources (CCRs) that were not identified?
- There are processes and resources out of control?

This means we need to add another aspect to the approach, an effective mechanism of control. The ability to know that an order is in danger of being late before we reach a point at which it is impossible or too expensive to correct and still be on time with the delivery.

STEP FIVE
Implementing buffer management

- Protect the constraint
- Identify the areas that are not in control

At this point we are able to get the best possible results from the system in its present state. We have learned to manage the system by identifying the constraint and applying the Five Focusing Steps. The measurements we have adopted allow us to assess to what degree we are achieving the goal which we established at the beginning.

However, we know that the processes of the system are naturally affected by variability and, as these processes act in a strictly interconnected way, this variability ends up influencing the performance of the constraint and therefore the Throughput of the system. It is important to understand that "one hour of the constraint is one hour of the system." We must always make sure the constraint works to the maximum of its possibilities in the time required.

How can we protect the constraint from the variability of the processes which impact it? We need a control mechanism. This mechanism must be capable of identifying the areas which are not in control and safeguarding the constraint's performance.

Let's consider what can normally happen in a company where we have planned the production by applying the Five Focusing Steps.

We have understood how we have to manage production, and have developed our plan in line with this. But when we have to deal with reality, things do not always go the way we expect. What happens if our plan comes up against out-of-control processes or behaviors that are not in line with the scheduling we have established? The mechanism we need must make us able to understand, before we get to a point of no return when it's too late to do anything about it, that an order is at risk of arriving late.

The Theory of Constraints solution is called buffer management. If we can identify the orders that are very likely to arrive late, and we have enough time to take corrective action, which allows us to put the situation right, then we have a better chance of shipping our orders on time. Buffer Management is the "look ahead" process that highlights when and where there is disruption in the flow. Buffer Management reduces the pressure on day-to-day expediting, and releases time for management to do more analysis and to learn what blockages are obstructing the flow. This analysis generates a positive feedback loop that strengthens the solution and creates an opportunity for further improvement.

Let's look at how the buffer works.

The unit of measurement of the buffer is time. As the aim of the buffer is to protect the constraint from the variability of the processes which feed it and which could "starve" it, we establish the length of the buffer on the basis of the variability of the processes which impact it. The greater the variability of the processes, the longer the buffer, and vice-versa. The look-ahead time buffer is used in order to identify problems and to initiate actions to overcome them, if and when needed. As the severity of a problem depends on the time that is left to recover from the problem, dividing the time buffer into three time zones (of equal size) is recommended. For each one of the zones there is a different set of managerial behaviors and operations.

A problem in a buffer is when we detect a disruption to the flow. In production such a disruption is manifested through the late arrival of materials, parts or products to a control point. When something is missing in a place where it is expected, we call it a "hole" in the buffer. In the case of production, we find for example the lack of finished products which according to our scheduling should have been ready. When we find "holes" in zone three (the farthest from the deadline date) we do not interfere in any way. People have enough authority and knowledge to deal with the situation. Every action we might take would be an act of tampering with the system.

In Zone II we begin to take notice. It's time to analyze what's going on so as to be ready to take corrective action. In Zone I we *must* take action at all costs so that orders are shipped on time, otherwise we lose Throughput.

Let's see how buffer management works in the production environment: The buffer controller visits the finished goods area and checks the number of finished goods ready to be shipped. Any unit which is not there is a missing one, and is called a "hole" in the buffer. The reaction to a "hole" depends on the amount of time left before the actual shipping date.

In Zone III we can expect to see holes in the buffer, as it takes time to travel from the Raw Materials (RM) to the Finished Goods (FG) areas.

In Zone II we expect to see some units arrive in the FG area. The only reason that a unit is not in the FG area is that it has been stopped on the way because of disruption to the flow. The buffer controllers can investigate where the missing units are. This will give them knowledge of the type of problems the units face on their way. For example, large batches, or a resource breakdown.

In Zone I immediate actions must be taken to rectify the situation and ensure shipping on time. (There is no need to say any more about this issue as all managers are experts in expediting to deliver on time—it's just regular fire-fighting.) The recording of arrivals of units to the FG area is demonstrated in the following graph.

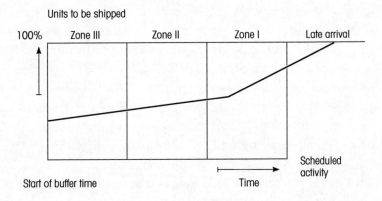

With better focusing and preventive actions created by Buffer Management we expect the graph to be changed to the following.

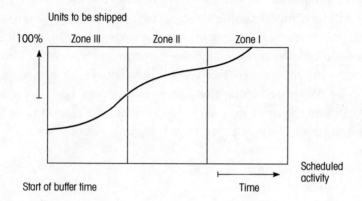

Project Management Using TOC

A project is a set of actions that are necessary to satisfy the specifications required by a customer. They must be carried out within a set time limit and budget.

What are the causes which prevent us from managing a project so it will be completed on time, within budget and within specs?

The core problem in project management is managing uncertainty. The way we absorb the variability of the things we do. Indeed, in spite of our tendency to inflate the estimates of the duration of the task by increasing the protection, we still don't manage to complete in time.

There are many different factors which cause us problems, but they all stem from the core problem of managing uncertainty. Let's look at some of these factors in particular.

1. Multi-tasking

The first way to handle multiple tasks is to perform each activity to completion in sequence (1–2–3.) In this case the "first" activity will be completed after a week, the "second" after two weeks and the "third" after three weeks. The second way is to split the work among the three activities—perform activities to 50% completion in sequence (1–2–3; 1–2–3). In this case the first activity will be completed in two weeks, the second in two and a half weeks and the third in three weeks. We call the second way bad multi-tasking. Nearly everybody loses and nobody wins.

2. Student syndrome

Let's look at the diagram below

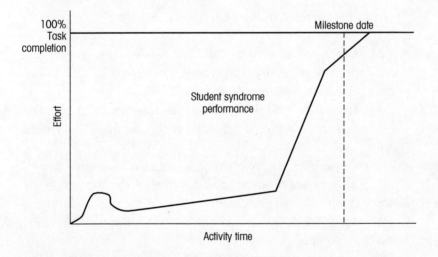

This diagram illustrates the so-called student syndrome. People's tendency to only really get moving to complete a task as the deadline approaches (the way students often start working on an assignment a few days before it is due). Clearly it is much more difficult to meet a deadline when you have to deal with unexpected events which crop up (the so-called Murphy's Law)

when you are forced to use all the capacity you have to carry out two-thirds of the project in the last third of the time allocated.

3. Interdependence of tasks

What happens when two (or more) tasks are interdependent and the first one finishes ahead of time? This "being early" does not get passed on to the next task. We never accumulate being early, only delays. And a delay on just one task means delaying the whole project.

In project management, when we consume time we consume our scarce resource, and that means losing money.

In order to manage effectively we have to complete projects on time, and so add protection to the various tasks. On the other hand, in order to manage effectively we have to make our organizations able to respond to customers promptly, and therefore not add protection to tasks.

There are various assumptions that connect the elements of the conflict. The assumption behind the two positions, add protection/don't add protection, is that all the tasks require protection.

The "injection" which allows us to solve this conflict is that it is not important to protect the individual activities which make up the project, but it is essential to protect the whole project. What does this mean? It means we must:

1. Add time at the end of the critical chain.
2. Define the critical chain as the longest sequence of activities considering simultaneously the dependence of the activities and the dependence of the resources.

In order to clarify better what we are saying, let's define what we mean by *critical path* and *critical chain*.

The critical path is defined as the longest path made up of dependent activities. The critical chain is defined as the longest sequence (time-wise) of dependent activities either of resources or of the path, taking into account the availability of resources.

How can we implement this solution? Which steps do we have to take?

If we analyze the definition of a project we gave previously, we see that we can also define a project as a set of interdependent activities which have to be completed respecting certain requirements. A project is a *system*.

We can therefore apply the Five Focusing Steps to Project Management, too. The approach is made up of the following five main steps.

Identify the constraint. What is the constraint of project management? The longest chain of dependent events (not only in a temporal sense but also considering the use of common resources) on which the duration of the project depends, also called the Critical Chain.

Exploit the Critical Chain. Do everything necessary to ensure that the key tasks are not behind schedule, including detailed planning. Safeguard the total time of the project and not the execution time of every single activity. To do this we put in the project buffer which protects the project conclusion date from fluctuations along the Critical Chain. The length of this buffer is initially 50% of the length of the Critical Chain. In fact the size of the project buffer depends on the variability of the interdependent processes. Clearly, this can only be done where there are control processes in place. Only *after* we have made our system stable can we apply the Five Focusing Steps to manage the organization, applying them to project management, production, or other areas.

In this stage we also insert the resource buffer which protects us from scarcity of resources. This guarantees that the resource we have allocated along the critical chain is present when it is needed. In order to activate the resource buffer mechanism we have two ways of operating.

1. We provide a kind of wake-up call to make sure the resource is available. In this way we alert the resource to act on tasks along the critical chain. This works when the system is very stable and everything happens as we expect it to.

2. We allocate an alternative resource. This makes sense when the tasks following the ones where we want to allocate the resource have a very high variability. In this case adding a resource means protecting the project completion date.

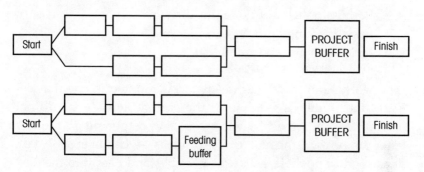

Subordinate. Subordinating everything else to the critical chain schedule determines the way we plan the non-critical parts of the project. The non-critical parts are called feeding chains, as they provide outputs that are essential for the integration with the critical chain or that feed a critical chain activity. Subordination means that the feeding activities are completed before the planned start of the critical activity. This is cause for the introduction of a feeding buffer.

The feeding buffer is there to protect us from the variability of the feeding activities. Its size depends on the level of variability. It is recommended to be initially at 50% of the length of the feeding chain. The feeding buffer is also instrumental in determining the earliest start to the feeding chain. Once we know the planned start of the critical chain activity we can backward schedule the feeding activities while inserting the feeding buffer.

Usually, there is no need to start earlier as it will increase investment, can cause disruption through request for change and does not give more protection as there is no need for more.

Subordination, in general, is the step that generates the majority of the short-term as well as the long-lasting benefits of the TOC approach. Planning can be done by few people (and in many cases can even be produced by a computer.) Successful implementation demands the synchronized efforts of many. The practicalities of the subordination include:

- Planning of the non-critical chain activities
- Permission to start non-critical chains
- Basic working attitude
- Measurements and mindset

The working attitude that needs to be adopted is one that negates the student syndrome. If the current attitude is "do not postpone until tomorrow what you can postpone until the day after tomorrow," the replacing attitude is—when I get a job, I do it as soon as possible, as fast as possible, and pass it to the next step. In TOC management jargon this is nicknamed the "Roadrunner" approach after the famous cartoon bird who stays put until it moves and then rapidly completes the task.

Another facet of subordination is the mindset of measurement. The prevailing mode of control is through the achievement of milestones within preplanned dates.

Whereas dates are a prime motivator for people as tangible objectives to be achieved and to be measured, they also have a negative effect. If there is slack time in the planning (which is usually the case even though people do not want to admit it), then the date is causing us to lose valuable time. This is time that we will not be able to use to protect the project from the variability in subsequent activities. The change required in the mindset is from "fix dates to deliver the output of an activity" into activity duration and the desire to finish as soon as possible and pass the work on.

Elevating the constraint. This is needed when the total duration of the project planned is too long and unacceptable for the customer. In order to reduce project duration we have to challenge parts of the project planning. Usually, doubling up of resources on the critical chain tends to have a good result. Other ideas include parallel processing and speeding up feeding chains.

Go back to Focusing Step 1. In project management this means the move from planning to execution. This is done through monitoring the buffers. Buffer management helps the managers involved in the project to anticipate problems before they cause major difficulties. Sorting out the problems ensures the smooth progression of the project while proper analysis of the core problem that endangers the successful completion of the project is carried out. Once a core problem is identified, a full cycle of identification of the solution and implementation of the solution should be employed. Last but not least, **the warning:** do not allow inertia to become a system constraint. There are many signs to indicate that after completion of the first four Focusing Steps people can be complacent and think or feel that everything is ok.

Statements like "It's always like that" and "What do you want, he is the best project manager we could find" signal dangerous inertia and introduce another dimension into project management. This is the need to deal with policy and human relationship constraints.

Multiple projects

When several projects are going on, the system we have to deal with consists of the set of various projects and the resources allocated to them. So we need to consider and therefore manage the interdependencies among the projects and the resources allocated to them. In this case what is our constraint? It is a critical resource that determines the fact that things are completed within the time established.

Let's call this resource strategic. The strategic resource determines the Throughput of the entire organization. If it is not working, the whole organization is losing Throughput.

Consequently, the strategic resource must be protected by a buffer—the strategic resource buffer. Where do we put this buffer? We put it in front of the task carried out by the strategic resource, in order to make sure the resource always has work to process. Generally speaking, there are three possible approaches for multi-project environments, depending on the context we are in.

1. Schedule all the projects together as if they were one big project.
2. Schedule incrementally. In this case we schedule one project at a time with the critical chain method, and every time we add a project we solve the conflicting needs for resources.
3. Schedule according to the critical resource. This is similar to the second approach except that the conflicting need for resources is solved only for the strategic resource and the first thing to be scheduled is the use of the strategic resource for all the projects.

If the buffers were simply a means of planning more effectively, it would be a good enough reason for using them. But there is a lot more to it. Buffers are an extremely valid tool for monitoring the state of a project and deciding which actions to take.

The buffers protect the project in its entirety by protecting the key scheduling areas. They can be used to predict the effects interruptions have on the project as a whole, which helps to solve many problems. By using buffers, managers acquire greater confidence in making and justifying their decisions.

Buffer management: conclusions

Buffer management provides us with a control mechanism which can protect the constraint and identify areas of the system which are not in control. If we want to get the maximum out of buffer management we must make sure that all the main processes which impact the constraint are stable, and have an interval of variability which allows them to be managed.

When we are dealing with a stable system that has a mechanism for controlling and protecting Throughput, we have in fact carried out the first three of the Five Focusing Steps. Now is the time to elevate the constraint.

STEP SIX
Reduce the variability of the constraint and the main processes

The Theory of Profound Knowledge and the Theory of Constraints were developed to guide and sustain a pattern of continuous improvement. We understand that this means creating the conditions for a continuous improvement of the company's limiting factor. Variability is the number one enemy. Less variability means more reliability, dependability, consistency. It means more Quality and better performances. This is precisely what we must pursue, starting from the constraint and the processes most closely connected to it.

Reducing the variability of stable processes is a difficult task because the forces acting on the system have achieved an intrinsic balance. No particular one is dominating. This should not by any means discourage us in our quest for better Quality. However, dealing with a stable system is definitely more cumbersome. Only well-planned experiments can lead us to discover the way to reduce variability and at the same time avoid tampering with the system.

We can use buffer management analysis to point out the areas that need attention:

- *Capacity constraints.* Not enough resources, lousy performance of resources, quality problems, and maintenance.
- *Policy and measurement constraints.* These lead people to take the wrong actions or not to take initiatives that could have moved the material faster.
- *Authority constraints.* When people have the responsibility for moving the material forward but do not have authority to solve difficulties and disruptions to the flow.
- *Sales constraints.* When orders are promised even though production is not capable of delivering all customers' expectations.
- *Human Relationship constraints.* Many times conflicts between individuals and departments prevent the removal of obstacles to the flow.

Buffer management can be seen as "problem generating" and "on-line policing." Therefore the buffer manager must have effective tools for problem solving and communication. The Thinking Processes enable us to deal with the vast majority of buffer management problems.

When we sort out the problems we have in Zone II, we get more consistent delivery with less holes in Zone I, which means that the amount of expediting is reduced dramatically. That is when we are ready to reduce the buffer time. Reducing buffer time reduces the manufacturing lead time and gives the company the opportunity to get more sales and increase Throughput.

At the same time, the reduction of buffer time will create more holes and send us on the quest for ongoing improvements. In a way, it sends us back to Focusing Step 1 as we have to identify the next constraint and start all over again.

There is one obstacle which we will certainly have to deal with while progressively reducing the variability of the constraint and the main processes of our system. This is the resistance to change that normally emerges in people. If we want to understand how to solve this problem, we have to ask ourselves what resistance to change actually means. Why do people resist change? Every solution is a change. Therefore every change should address the three basic questions presented in our introduction. What to change? What to change to? How to make the change happen? If the answers to the above questions do not match people's intuition or logic, then the whole "package" is rejected.

If we want our solution to be implemented successfully, then all those involved have to be able to adapt their way of behaving to the requirements of that solution. For this to happen, people in the organization have to understand the change which is being asked of them.

What we have to do is develop and communicate the solution in such a way that:

- It corresponds to people's logic.
- Step by step everyone is involved in its construction.

Goldratt has distinguished six levels of resistance to change. For each level there is a corresponding Thinking Process, or set of Thinking Processes.

Layer One: Disagreement about the problem ("It's not my problem.")

To be able to overcome this hurdle we must pinpoint the core problem that is responsible for the majority of the negative effects that exist in our reality.

As people have good intuition, they must have a fair perception of what a core problem is. However, they cannot remove the core problem, or, sometimes they do not dare to address it because there are conflicting powers that force the continuous existence of the core problem.

The mechanism employed is the construction of the core problem cloud as described in Chapter 5. The outcome of the process is a clear understanding of the power conflict or management dilemma that fuels the core problem.

When presenting the core problem cloud, it is not sufficient to create consensus on the problem. Another tool is used—the Current Reality Tree—to communicate the logic supporting the identification of the core problem.

At this stage we have achieved consensus on the problem. It should be clear to everyone by now what the problem is and, even if the problem appears before us in all its difficulty, we are ready to do something about it.

Layer Two: Disagreement about the direction of the solution

Layer One is overcome when all the relevant parties involved in the area of improvement have agreed that the *core problem cloud* (CP-Cloud) is a fair and correct presentation of their reality. The CP-Cloud also explains the instability imposed on their behavior and decision-making and the emotional frustration caused by the instability.

The increasing emotion associated with the core problem creates the need for a direction for the solution, something that will tell us that there is a way out. The *injection* that breaks the core problem provides the direction for the solution. Layer Two is supposed to provide us with a way out. The emotional reaction to Layer Two must be one of relief; the pressure of the core problem cloud should go down.

Clouds do not always have "class solutions." This means that there will not always be only one suggested injection. There can also be situations in which no injection is found by the parties participating in the process. In this case they just have to think harder.

The most important outcome of the process is that the overall situation changes from "you against me because of the problem" to "you and me against the problem."

Layer Three: Lack of faith in the completeness of the solution

In this case, there is a mismatch in the comprehension of the change and the logic that brings the results. The *Future Reality Tree* (FRT) is where we gather all the supporting logic to "prove" why we claim that the proposed change will bring results. But there are more objectives that the FRT has to help achieve. It has to help us to identify more injections that are needed in order to realize the benefits. It helps us to round the solution and to bring it to a simple, practical and comprehensible state.

Layer Four: Fear of negative consequences generated by the solution

People have good intuition. Intuition stems from experience. Experience is stored in our databank. Therefore, sometimes an idea seems to us "not such a good one." How do we know? It is because we have had a lousy experience with such an idea. It is like the way young children learn. How do they know to be wary of hot things? Once they touch a hot thing and feel pain, they develop the instinct not to touch hot things again.

If people have had the experience of an improvement initiative causing job redundancies, their intuition will tell them to watch out so they do not improve themselves out of their jobs.

This is an extreme case. But many times people want to inform the initiator that something negative can be the result if the change is successfully integrated.

Dealing properly with the negative response is necessary for three main objectives.

- To protect and immunize the proposed change from unexpected difficulties (snakes in the grass).
- To get the buy-in of the people who tend to be devil's advocates.

- To demonstrate leadership through listening and incorporating relevant input.

The Thinking Process (TP) tool is called the *Negative Branch Reservation* (NBR).

Layer Five: Too many obstacles along the road that leads to the change

The good news about reaching Layer Five is that we are closer to the introduction of the new ideas into our reality. In this layer the reservations and comments we hear are about obstacles standing in the way. Usually they are about resources. "We don't have money; we don't have time; we have so many projects to run; my people can't understand it; my boss will never agree."

As with NBR, listening is of great value in bringing about change. It may highlight difficulties we were not aware of and which could hurt us when we want to introduce the change to our reality. The process of handling Layer Five also involves facilitating individuals in the releasing of their intuition, and it provides us with the building blocks of the relevant knowledge.

The people who raise the obstacle reservations are, in most cases, the most qualified people to suggest the way to overcome the obstacles. They have the experience, the intuition and they care. Otherwise, why would they bother to signal to us that there is an obstacle?

We must find a solution for every major obstacle, otherwise the obstacle will block us from moving forward and achieving the benefits from the change. How many initiatives have you personally experienced in the last few years that have not materialized and that have left you and others disillusioned or cynical about the applicability of implementing any improvement initiative? All of this has happened because many obstacles, especially the critical ones, have been ignored or not handled properly.

We call the solution for an obstacle an *Intermediate Objective* (IO) This is when the obstacle no longer stands in the way of change. Usually there is more than one way to overcome the obstacle. The IO-Map draws the logical connections of all the necessary prerequisites that must be achieved. This is why the IO-Map is also called a *Prerequisite Tree* (PRT).

Layer Six: Not knowing what to do

When Layer Five has been overcome there are very few reasons left for not getting on with the solution. Individuals have been assigned responsibilities, and they have raised all their concerns in the concensus process of Layer Five, and all of them have been handled by the team or by the leader. This is the right situation to take actions and make things happen.

Nevertheless, we find many cases in which people do not move. Usually, it is because they do not know how to proceed, and do not feel comfortable about asking for more detailed directions. If they are open about it we will have an easier entry into Layer Six. Otherwise we may be fighting windmills or ghosts. To overcome Layer Six we have to ensure that every individual is not blocked on a personal basis. People may not raise their real concerns in Layer Five, and some personal obstacles may catch up with us in Layer Six.

There are several methods for overcoming Layer Six.

If people do not move after Layer Five, then the leader must take actions to move them. This is when leadership is critical.

- Obtain clear instructions from a person who has the knowledge of performing the activity, and transfer this know-how to the person who is expected to perform it.
- Develop a detailed plan to achieve an ambitious Intermediate Objective (IO).
- Address the Intermediate Objective assigned to the per-

son as an ambitious target on its own, and repeat the
Layer Five process.
- Address the IO as a full subject matter and develop it
  from Layer One to Layer Six.
- Convert the initiative into a project and manage it using
  the Critical Chain approach to project management.
- Deal with individuals who do not perform by using a
  subset of the Thinking Processes that the manager can
  use for handling individuals' difficulties.

The Thinking Processes tools represent a valid support in
overcoming the levels of resistance we encounter when we try to
develop a solution. In addition we need an organizational mechanism that manages the improvement of the system constantly,
and that develops complete solutions based on logic and common sense. In other words, we need a suitable management
structure.

Chapter 3

Making the System Grow

Steps 7–10

STEP SEVEN
Creating a suitable management structure

Let's go back to what we learned in Step 2. The hierarchical structure is inspired by a concept of the company in which every individual is the only person who carries out and is responsible for the activities assigned to him/her. This way of thinking leads us to the conclusion that the overall result equals the sum of the contributions of single individuals and functions.

The measurement system and the rewards system strictly linked to it were developed according to this logic. This means that individuals and departments are measured on the basis of their local performance, which takes on an intrinsic value, and not according to the impact their actions have on the goal of the system.

Not everyone is aware of the extent to which performance assessment methods affect people's behavior in the organization. "Tell me how you measure me and I'll tell you how I'll behave." So, if we insist on adopting a management structure based on the hierarchical model, we will meet enormous difficulties when we try to manage our system according to the Five Focusing Steps and we have to subordinate the rest of the system to the decision we have made regarding the constraint.

Let's look at this more closely. If we subordinate every other component of the system to the decisions made about the constraint, and the constraint is really the constraint, then all the rest of the system will have to restrain itself from producing to the maximum.

For example, the following diagram represents the organizational structure of a company with five departments. The numbers inside the boxes represent the capacity that each department has to process customer orders. Customer orders flow from left to right. The numbers between the boxes reflect the number of customer orders that are stuck in between departments (work in progress).

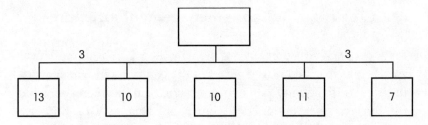

In this diagram it is obvious that the fifth department (the extreme right box) is the constraint—the limiting factor for the company Throughput.

We have to decide how to exploit it and we have to subordinate everything else to this. This means not only that this box cannot waste one second, but every other performance in every other box has to be designed to make the maximum out of it. The only maximum performance which makes sense is the one processed by the constraint.

If the chosen constraint is a real one, then, by definition, every other box will have more capacity; this means that all the other boxes will have to refrain from "making the maximum." The only meaningful "maximum" can only be what the constraint can absorb.

Unfortunately, under the prevailing performance appraisal systems, this would mean a poor rating. The individual efficiency of the boxes would be considered too low and the "excess capacity" bound to be trimmed. In other words, people working in the non-constraint boxes would be punished for doing what makes sense.

If we assess this kind of performance in the traditional way, then the result will be terrible. People will be reprimanded for not having "done their best." So what will happen is that, in order to avoid being punished, people will adapt the pace of their work to that of the constraint.

What is the outcome of this attitude? The system will take on the behavior of the straight tube with the perfectly constant diameter which we looked at in Step Four of The Decalogue. As we saw, it turned into a series of connected bottlenecks, and the manager's reaction will be consistent with the traditional management methods.

If we continue to act on the system by ignoring the constraint and managing the organization according to a hierarchical model, we will never manage to break free, and we will go on moving in a vicious cycle.

The hierarchical model is equally unsuitable when we apply the Theory of Constraints to project management. This goes for single projects as well as multi-projects.

Indeed, as we have seen, when we insert a resource in single projects it can lead to a conflict, due to the fact that adding a resource takes us over budget. We can solve this conflict by realizing that the only budget we have to protect is that of the company, not of individual functions.

What happens, though, when we apply TOC in a multi-project situation? What are the repercussions on the structure of our organization? In an environment where several projects using shared resources are managed simultaneously, we have to do a shared scheduling. But most of all we must take into consideration the interdependencies among the resources. We gain considerable advantages this way: the more global the scheduling, the shorter the buffers and project completion time. This happens because:

1. We pool all the protection needed in the buffers, thus reducing completion time.
2. The priorities are clearer.
3. There is less confusion.
4. There is greater productivity.

Moreover, if we don't consider the interdependencies we become more vulnerable to a widespread problem in our companies which stems from a hierarchical vision of organizations: squabbling over resources.

In a multi-project environment a particular resource could be considered strategic: if a resource determines the Throughput of the organization it in fact becomes the constraint. It is also true that there are "problematic" resources which are not strategic, but could temporarily become constraints. They should be identified as such and kept under control. We have to eliminate temporary constraints.

There are many reasons why planning in multi-project environments is very complicated. One of the main reasons is that the level of synchronization and communication necessary among project managers, resource managers and staff is difficult if not impossible to achieve in organizations which are managed hierarchically.

If we look again at the three approaches we already saw for managing multi-projects using TOC (scheduling everything together, scheduling successive projects, managing strategic buffers) we realize that whichever of the three approaches we choose, we will always have to deal with a series of needs which will clash with the hierarchical model of management: we must solve or minimize squabbling over resources; replace traditional control mechanisms for work progress (in favor of buffer management); make available updated information for all project managers; and cause flexibility and visibility of the interdependencies of the system.

The examples of application of TOC to production and Project Management have taught us that a hierarchical structure has created two fundamental problems.

1. People have a very limited view of their jobs.
2. It is practically impossible to allocate and manage resources bearing in mind the overall goal of the organization.

If we want to implement a systemic Deming-Goldratt-based management approach in a way which allows us to achieve results and long-term improvement, we have to create a suitable managerial structure. This is an extremely difficult step to take. However, once we have gotten this far, we have everything we need to be able to make it happen.

- We have the Thinking Processes to bring about a change of this magnitude.
- By this stage in our transformation we have concrete results to show. This means that our authority is reinforced and we are able to go ahead.

The conflict of hierarchy versus system

As the conflict between a hierarchical and systemic vision of organizations has never been as evident as it is now, let's "evaporate" it, i.e., solve it. Let's set out the elements of the conflict.

In order to manage our organization effectively we must be able to see the interdependencies of the system and therefore we must manage our organization according to the systemic model. We have seen the logic which inspires the systemic management of organizations.

On the other hand, in order to manage effectively we must

have control over the organization and therefore we must manage it according to the hierarchical model. Why? Because if we divide up our organization into so many boxes, we can exercise control over each one and over the whole thing.

The need which the hierarchical model protects is the need for control. If we find another way of controlling the system that does not require adopting the hierarchical model, there will no longer be valid reasons for continuing to manage organizations hierarchically.

Indeed, the complexity of our organizations prevents us from controlling and acting on the part of the organization we are responsible for. All the various functions are so closely interlinked that we cannot seriously think that the performance of one individual function is completely independent from the rest of the system. Consequently, it is impossible to think of having the whole organization under control with a mechanism of this kind.

If we look at the organization from a systemic point of view, we realize that in order to control our system's performance we do not need to keep every single component under control. It's enough to control the factor which limits the Throughput of the system—the constraint. We know how to do that—*buffer management*.

At this point we have the elements for creating a managerial structure that is in keeping with the approach we have so far constructed. This structure will support making Deming's scheme operational.

The new structure drastically improves the system of interactions, and this allows us to make coherent and synchronized decisions about the functioning of the system. The people in the organization, as well as being sufficiently empowered, gain new motivation for working toward the goal of the system because their behavior is not influenced by misguided incentive systems. The management, the staff, the resources and processes are all in a position to be able to satisfy the goal of the system.

STEP EIGHT
Eliminating the external constraint: selling the excess capacity

Excess capacity

At this point we should not be surprised if the constraint has moved outside the company. As we have seen, TOC addresses the limiting factor of the system—the constraint. If we apply the Five Focusing Steps adequately, the constraint will soon shift to outside our organization. At this point the constraint will become the willingness of the market to buy everything we can produce.

What happens in this situation? If the market does not absorb all our products, and we do not want to fill our warehouses with accumulated inventory, we should reduce production. When we reduce production, people have less work to do; the work can be done by fewer people. Many people in recent years have come to the conclusion that a company can get by with a smaller staff. This line of reasoning has led to a policy of reducing staff as a means of cost-cutting in order to increase profits. In this way the people who contributed to improving the company get rewarded with being fired.

What is the assumption behind the paradoxical thinking that the more a system improves, the fewer people it needs?

Once again, it is the thinking tied to a hierarchical vision. The pursuit of local optimization at the cost of overall results of the system, focusing on cutting costs instead of increasing Throughput.

The answer at this point in our transformation process should be pretty clear. It lies in using and applying the Profound Knowledge that Deming theorized. Only when we constantly analyze and reason about the processes of our organization, and take actions to reduce variation and stabilize our system do we realize how important it is to have excess capacity. It is only by accepting the paradigm which TOC represents—moving from the cost world to the Throughput world—that we succeed in focusing on the *real* improvement of our system's performance.

Then we have to manage a new kind of constraint, an external constraint. In this case, we must subordinate to the new constraint: sales. If we manage to sell our excess capacity, thus generating further Throughput, we will have found the way to make our system perform to its maximum. Let's focus on the way we sell.

Understanding Customers

The customer is the most important link in the chain. This is what Dr. Deming used to say. Accordingly, a successful organization must have a built-in mechanism in the way it operates that allows it to understand and satisfy the needs of the customer. We believe that the most spectacular application of the power of the Tools resides in addressing the market.

What is the criterion that drives people to buy a product?

It is the value they believe their purchase will give them. We might even say that buying a product takes the purchaser from an "undesirable" situation to a "desirable" one.

We can get people's perception of the value of our product to increase enormously if we can make them see that it solves a problem for them.

If we identify our present and potential customers' problems, their Undesirable Effects or UDEs, we can find the core problem, the source from which they derive.

TOC claims that UDEs are not independent; they are all connected and they all, ultimately, stem from a common source. We call this source the "core problem." TOC also provides us with a powerful way to derive a core problem quickly and systematically, given a set of UDEs. We call this the CRT (Current Reality Tree).

It is possible, then, given a number of UDEs, to derive the core problem from which they all originate. Needless to say, if we tackle the core problem successfully, all the UDEs will either disappear or their negative impact will be reduced drastically.

So, making offers to the market in a way that substantially increases their chance of being accepted starts with addressing not so much the individual UDEs themselves, but the way they lead us to the core problem from which they originate.

If we know our potential clients' core problem, we are definitely more likely to formulate offers which will be accepted by them.

As we have already said, the customer's perception of the product's value is linked to the way it tackles the core problem.

If this is true, what is essential for us to know in order to make an offer? The undesirable effects. Why? Because in this way we can derive the core problem! In order to do this we stratify the data we have concerning our clients. The criteria we use to put them into categories is the commonality of the UDEs.

Stratifying data means, in essence, sorting data into homogeneous categories, categories that have something in common. The "something" is the *rationale* inspiring the stratification.

We need to go through this exercise if we want to be successful with our customers. The knowledge gained will provide us with the element needed to produce a winning offer. A valuable offer must be perceived as such. It must contain elements that allow the prospect to understand its value, but it must also eliminate any doubt about its chance of being accepted.

Are we saying that our database of clients should have a field called main UDEs? Yes, we are. Are we saying that when we build a mailing list we should subgroup our addresses according to common main UDEs? Yes, we are. When we group organizations according to their UDEs we are able to develop common core conflicts. As we shall see, the core problem of a prospect is the assumption lying behind his/her core conflict; this assumption is the reason that prevents him/her from buying what we offer.

Similar core conflicts may have slightly different underlying assumptions and therefore require different injections. However, as we are in a situation of excess capacity, it is very likely that we have the resources to implement all these injections.

Before we do that, we must ascertain that the injections found do evaporate all the UDEs. Not only that. The injections found must replace the UDEs with the corresponding Desirable Effect, and must not generate new UDEs. The TP tool necessary for this is called the Future Reality Tree (FRT).

If we recognize the importance of this way of thinking, the next step is: how I am going to make a prospect like my offer so much that he/she is going to accept it? We shall call this kind of offer "unrefusable," meaning that no prospect would ever dream of refusing it. An offer that is extremely convenient for the buyer and the seller.

However, to present such an offer requires some preliminary work; unfortunately, even win-win offers do not sell themselves.

This means we have to construct an offer that contains all the ingredients that allow a customer to understand the value of the product we're offering (that we're offering a solution to their core problem). But we also have to find a way to eliminate any doubt they may have that our offer will not materialize.

If we use the TOC Thinking Processes Tools in full, we will be able to:

- Properly exploit the knowledge provided by a correct stratification.
- Fully understand the customer's need.
- Increase our chance of satisfying the customer.

Guidelines for constructing a marketing offer

A good solution is one that solves problems. The more problems the solution solves, the better. Therefore, an offer that solves a core problem is something that solves many problems. The customer will latch onto such a solution.

This is good, but not enough. As we know, the major difficulty with sorting out core problems is that individuals or organizations have to change. If we can find a solution that does not require the customer to change, it will be even more attractive. This means that we have to cause the change on *our* side.

We also have to protect such an offer. We all know that when we come up with a new offer, our competitors will copy it in a very short period of time, and we will lose the window of opportunity created by the new offer. This is why price reduction is not a proper marketing offer. Our competitors can copy it overnight, and we all lose.

What can we change that our competitors will have difficulty changing? The answer is policy constraints. Policies are not easy to change. You need courageous leaders with a great deal of support from their people.

Once we have such an offer we want to consider our side as well. We do not only want to win the orders. We would like to get a premium price for the additional value we bring to our customers.

Summary: A marketing offer has the following characteristics:

- Addresses a core problem of the customer.
- Does not demand them to change—the supplier changes.
- Ideally, it breaks a policy constraint of the supplier.
- It provides the supplier with a potential price increase.

Constructing the unrefusable marketing offer

1. Collect problems from your clients—the problems that prevent them from doing a good job or achieving their objectives.
2. Check that these problems are causing quantifiable damage to their performance, like lost Throughput, increased operating expense.
3. Select three major problems that cause heavy "pain."
4. Develop a conflict diagram (the cloud explained in Chapter 5) for each one of these problems.

5. Create a general conflict diagram that consolidates the elements of the individual problems.
6. Identify plausible reasons for causing the conflict and choose one that you or your company can assist in eliminating. This will be the need of your customer that your offer addresses in such a way that they will not be able to turn it down.
7. Develop a full solution to ensure benefits to your customer without creating negative outcomes for you or your company.

Once you have an agreed solution, the offer has to be checked internally to see that it is not only logical, but practical and does not carry negative branches. There is definitely a strong need for consensus and support from the top and from the people who will have to carry it out.

Thereafter, it has to be packaged well and sales people will have to learn how to sell it and develop a process to continuously improve their abilities to sell.

STEP NINE
Bringing the constraint inside the organization when possible

By this stage, the organization has gained the experience and the benefits of addressing most of the constraints one can expect to find in any organization. The major types of constraints are:

- Resource and capacity constraints
- Time constraints
- Policy constraints
- Sales constraints
- Marketing constraints
- Organization (structure) constraints
- Human behavior constraints

For some types of constraints there are generic solutions that contain breakthrough ideas which can set the direction. These solutions have been implemented since 1975 and have been proven to be successful. They produce the expected results.

A generic solution must, of course, be customized for every specific environment. However, the fact that a generic solution exists is of great assistance, as it saves us from re-inventing the wheel every time.

Resource and capacity constraints are addressed through the use of the Drum-Buffer-Rope (DBR) approach. Drum-Buffer-Rope helps in identifying what generates unwanted variability in the production line. DBR used in conjunction with Buffer Management (BM) allows effective exploitation of the constraint, as well as control over the performance of the system.

Time constraints which are critical for product development, projects and improvement initiative, are addressed, controlled and elevated through the concepts of critical chain, synchronization of strategic resources (drum) and buffer management.

Policy constraints need to be dealt with through the use of the Thinking Processes. These provide the tools for systematic analysis of the following three elements.

- The core policy, which is responsible for the majority of the negative symptoms.
- A new policy to replace it, which is simple, practical and that sorts out many of the negative symptoms and replaces them with positive effects.
- A way to integrate the new policy into the company in such a way that if it is used, generates the expected benefits and does not have any negative implications.

One example of a policy constraint for which there is a generic solution is the distribution policy, based on having stocks in strategic locations along the path from the manufacturer to the end consumer. The policy constraint causes shortages, over-stocking, waste and lousy customer service. The TOC replenishment solution allows the whole supply-chain to respond quickly to the real demand in the market, while holding an overall lower inventory.

Measurements, policies and procedures are mechanisms that force people to perform in a certain way. They determine the "rules" of the organization. These rules also dictate and control the way people behave. In addition, the organizational structure is geared to support the direction the company has been going in. However, when the goal of the organization becomes improvement, the rules for running it must be adapted and adjusted to an ever-changing environment. The problem is that there are always people within the organization who may feel threatened due to the change. As a result, they will enforce the old rules as if they had been written in stone.

Sales constraints are the constraints concerning the ability of the salespeople to close deals. Addressing this constraint requires salespeople to redirect their mind-set and become very focused on the objective they are asked to achieve—to sell! It is about mind-set, determination and demonstration of commitment to the goal of the company, even if that entails some personal inconveniences when it comes to changing personal perspectives and paradigms.

Marketing constraints are addressed through the development of a special offer that the market cannot refuse. As we have seen in Step Eight, having brought the system into a high level of stability has allowed a proper maximization of its Throughput via the use of Drum-Buffer-Rope and Buffer Management.

Organization (structure) constraints arise when the developing business is held back by practices, functions and authorities that do not make sense anymore. Once again the Thinking Processes have to be used in order to develop a new structure that will fit the growing business. There are few models of organizational structure which fit the continuous growth of an organization. Nevertheless, if the organization has passed through Step Seven of The Decalogue, it means that the leaders already have proven that they have the courage to address tough constraints, even if that means slaughtering sacred cows.

The human behavior constraint has been addressed throughout the whole Decalogue: setting the goal, defining measurements, designing and making the system stable and controlling variation. The major cause for variation and the existence of the constraints is human behavior. We can say that the deepest constraint is: *The resistance to addressing the constraint!*

By implementing the first eight steps of The Decalogue, the organization has gone through the experience of addressing constraints. Constraint is no longer a dirty word. Indeed, it is the key to growth; it is right for the organization as a whole and it is right for every individual who has gone through the process.

With the experience and the incredible confidence the organization has built, there is nothing to stop it from continuously improving. There is only one question left.

Where do you want the organization constraint to be?

We have stated that a constraint is a positive part of our life. With the Five Focusing Steps and the Thinking Processes we can manage the organization and all its parts effectively.

At the same time, we know that every system must have a constraint. There must always be a weakest link (even if it is a strong chain that can carry many tons of weight).

As we know how to address every constraint, and as there always should be a constraint, the question is: Which constraint is our preference? To answer that question we have to ask ourselves another question. Is it better to have an internal constraint or an external one?

External means that the people and organizations involved are not a part of our own organization. It means that we do not have any authority, and therefore the ability to control the constraint is totally dependent on our ability to influence and to provide win-win solutions. The process is not completely under our control. There can be outside influences that are beyond our control.

However, the internal constraints are, instead, under our control. Therefore, ideally we would like to have an internal constraint. And of all the constraints, why not choose the one that is simple, easy to manage, and does not create any hassle or emotion—the *capacity constraint?*

Ideally, having a capacity constraint is healthy. We would like to have one resource or one department that is the strategic constraint. Focusing Step 2 ensures that we produce the right product mix, and Focusing Step 3 guarantees an excellent return from the use of the constraint.

The constraint should be loaded to only 95% capacity, so we can leave some demand for the competition, as we do not want to kill them completely and create a monopoly. Continuous improvement should be done in controlled steps of increasing capacity while increasing demand. As the organization should be, by now, in an outstanding financial position, it can sustain short periods of a small excess in capacity before the sales catch up.

There are few examples of organizations that have grown continuously through the use of this process (as opposed to those who have achieved growth through acquisitions).

Continuous improvement—real life showcases

Usually, the graph representing the financial performance of a company looks like a very nervous drawing, with ups and downs and fluctuations. Not all performances live up to the expectations of the five-year plans. Recently we were involved in a company whose net profit graph in the years between 1987 and 1997 looked like this.

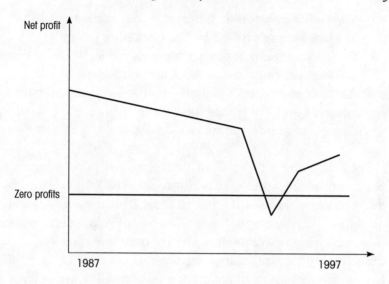

This is definitely not a good example of continuous improvement. The graph shows us a continuous decline in the profit of the organization. Whatever actions were taken did not work. Being a subsidiary of a big company, the pressure from headquarters to improve was immense. In the period between 1990 and 1996 three managing directors were replaced and sales directors were fired. However, the sliding trend did not stop.

On the basis of the poor business performance, the board of directors had decided to downsize the company. This decision caused immediate industrial relationship problems that led to further commercial losses. The managing director was fired and an external consultant was brought in. The consultant managed to salvage the situation and bring the company out of the red. Within a year the company was sold to a capital venture group.

The objective of The Decalogue is to prevent such situations, and to correct those that are already going in the wrong direction. We have to remember that "you can ignore the constraint, but the constraint will not ignore you."

The analysis of the company presents a combination of several severe constraints.

- *Marketing constraint.* Change in the marketplace that has not been addressed by the marketing policy.
- *Policy constraint.* Looking inwards rather than to the market; focusing on cost reduction initiatives.
- *Attitude constraint.* Continual battles between top management and the troops, leading to lack of trust, confidence and support in times of crisis.

The consultant who came in 1995 managed to help the company improve their delivery performance. The WIP was dramatically reduced through the use of basic DBR concepts, and the on-time delivery improved. The improved performance regained customer confidence, and the company came out of the crisis. Now they are addressing the real constraints, and they have a greater chance of continuing their positive growth. As it is a seasonal business, their activity tends to tail off in December and does not pick up again until April. December 1998 and the first quarter of 1999 were the best they had for many years and many jobs were saved. Had the company not grown, costs, and therefore jobs would have been cut.

Stagnation and deterioration

Stagnation or deterioration in the performance of a company is caused by a constraint (or several interactive constraints). The purpose of the last part of the Decalogue (Steps 7 to 10) is to ensure that, after the initial success, management strives to search for the next constraint and to address it.—(Focusing Step Five of the TOC approach, when a constraint is broken go back to Focusing Step One.)

The "single constraint approach" is manifested in the financial performance as:

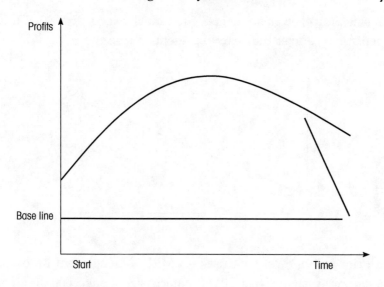

Many improvement initiatives produce such benefits. Very few companies can present a steady growth in profits over many years that originates from improvement initiatives. One of the showcases on continuous improvement using TOC is Valmont Industries.

A real example of Process of Ongoing Improvement (POOGI)—Valmont Industries

In March 1998, in a TOC Conference in San Antonio, Texas, USA, Allen Abney and Roger Caldwell gave a presentation entitled *It Just Can't Be This Simple*.

This is the story of Valmont, a company that has been consistent in its use of TOC for over eleven years. They managed to balance the improved production with additional sales. This has ensured that they did not have to oscillate between internal and external constraints. It is an outstanding example of a company that managed to keep the constraint inside the company, utilizing their capacity constraint to its maximum level, and controlling the amount of investment in elevating the constraint (Focusing Step 4) so as not to create too much excess capacity. Their performance over the years represents a true POOGI.

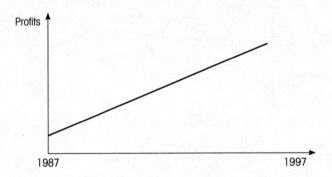

Prior to 1987, Valmont used an MRP (Management Resource Planning) system. Their bill of materials contains 8,000 different part numbers. Through control listing, they predetermined and set batch quantity to minimize set-ups and maximize efficiency throughout the shop. Based on MRP, they scheduled all shipping items with a Monday ship date, and then MRP backward-scheduled the ship date.

Due to batches starting every week, they had a lot of hours at the end of the prior week. They generated schedules to keep capacity leveled throughout the entire shop and still maintain the pre-determined level of efficiency and productivity. The fill-up and weld areas were the constraints, and the total capacity experienced problems on MRP.

Pre-determined batch sizes caused big queues. Priorities were set on orders with the least amount of shortages, resting on orders that were the latest on the shop. They experienced a lot of expediting due to late week starts, past due orders grew, rescheduling became the norm.

Then in 1987, Jeff Wood gave copies of Eli Goldratt's book *The Goal* to the staff and asked for everyone's opinion. Everyone thought the book was talking about Valmont. They realized that some change had to take place. But they were faced with one big question. Would we have to eliminate all existing systems and start all over again, or could we interface the two together?

They also realized that for this change to be effective, a new mindset needed to be developed. They realized that all their efforts would not mean anything if they were not tied to the constraint. Set-ups, efficiencies, batch sizes meant nothing if not tied to the goal.

They implemented DBR. The Drum was the finite schedule of the system's constraint, and the Buffer was time protection for the constraint against any disruption. The Rope was the releasing of raw material to the shop floor.

They witnessed the processing time become significantly shorter than the customer quoted lead-time. They launched their order to the constraint based on the start date, then used MRP to forward-schedule the finish date.

They scheduled the subordinate area based on the finish date and allowed MRP to backward-schedule the start date.

They allowed some machines to sit idle as long as they were not the constraints. But they still measured the constraint by traditional methods. They implemented Buffer Management next, and they established a CCR analysis report to show where there were buffer holes in the system.

In the following plant diagram, CCR 1495 (fill-up) and CCR 0139 (weld area) are the constraints. The planned buffer content consists of three zones: Zone 1 (days 1 and 2), Zone 2 (days 3 and 4) and Zone 3 (days 5 and 6). They are 100% complete, approximately 70% complete and 30% complete, respectively.

All parts required for the constraint for day 1 and day 2 must be completed as inventory by the beginning of the shift, which is day 1. Any buffer hole in Zone 1 must take priority. It must stay 100% all the time. They have six days of buffer in front of the constraint. Careful observation of these buffers can tell us a great deal about the inevitable fluctuations in our plant and its marketplace.

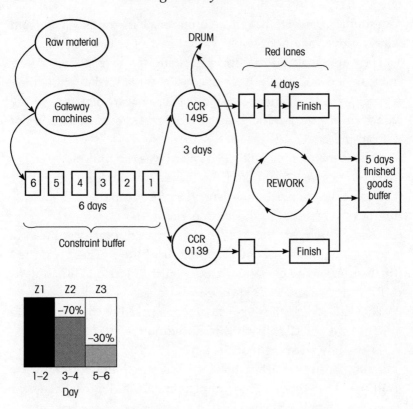

Rework area

The rejected items are important, as they have already consumed the constraint time. They take top priority, as wasted
bottleneck time is lost Throughput for the plant. These items
don't go back to the constraint, as that is physically impossible.

They established a CCR constraint analysis report for the subordinate areas. This report tells them where to track all buffer
holes in Zone 1 every day. This provides some history of what is
the major Zone 1 buffer hole violator.

They were successful because they were able to generate the
paradigm shift needed; to tell them how they were actually being measured, e.g., buffer hole in their department.

After implementing TOC, Throughput increased from 8.5M (1986) to 46.5M (1996).

Before they attempted to eliminate the strategic constraints, they used the CCR buffer analysis to find out what were the number 1 and number 2 major Zone 1 buffer violators. They knew that if they elevated the constraint, Zone 1 major buffer violators were going to create problems. Therefore the CCR report was to locate these areas and make improvement there. They also looked behind the constraint to find out what chronically gave them problems after a part had left the constraint.

They were able to keep the constraint in-house by making sure the bottleneck would not move as they elevated the constraint. They paid a lot of attention to the machines that created holes in Zone 1 and, if touched, would cause the constraint to move.

They have constantly maintained the buffer size over the past eleven years by:

1. Realizing that expanding or reducing the buffer does not bring any advantage to the company in terms of getting more sales.
2. Constantly increasing production volume, and instead of expanding or fluctuating the buffer, holding it at a fixed size—6 days.

They realized that the focus of the company is essential, and there are areas that can disrupt their focus, including playing around with the oscillations of the buffer size, and if the constraint does not stay where it is.

They decided the level of constraint buffers according to the constraint capacity that the market dictates. And they added capacity to the red lane without touching the constraints. Only recently, they elevated the constraint capacity by 10% with just a few thousand dollars of investment. However they were careful enough so that this was done without increasing the capacity everywhere. The benefits of doing so were impressive.

Indeed, they have always based their business decisions on the Throughput, Inventory and Operating Expenses of the company, and continuously apply the Five Focusing Steps in their operation. The effort to maintain buffers and increase the bottleneck capacity (while still keeping it a bottleneck) on an ongoing basis is one essence of success for Valmont. They shifted their focus from just reducing the most important disruptions to also increasing Throughput at the bottlenecks. That is called the productivity flywheel.

The second most important factor of their successful implementation of TOC is the workforce's paradigm. It has been changed to adapt well to change. They have brought the entire group to view the process of Ongoing Improvement in the same light, and to embrace it together.

STEP TEN
Set up a continuous learning program

The real voyage of discovery consists not in seeking
new landscapes,
but in having new eyes.
—A la recherche du temps perdu, Marcel Proust

The only missing element we have in order to embark on a process of continuous improvement is continuous learning. An organization has to realize that to achieve its goal—to improve—it must embark on the process and the mindset of continuous learning. This is the essence of Step 10.

As we saw earlier, the very nature of organizations as systems interacting with their surrounding environment exposes them to change.

External reality continues to change at a hectic pace and more and more we have to guarantee the system is working properly and achieving its goal. This means we have to ensure a mechanism is in place that allows us to generate and up-date the knowledge we need in order to manage the system.

This mechanism can be found in the continuous learning cycle that Deming called PDSA and which we saw in Step Three of our Decalogue.

TOC provides us with a tool that allows us to plan out the actions for continuous improvement and transform the undesirable effects we experience into desirable ones. It also allows us to check that our actions are effective, and make sure new undesirable effects don't crop up. This tool is the Future Reality Tree (FRT).

The systemic nature of the FrT can also be seen by the fact that it contains a feedback mechanism (the equivalent of the ACT—step 4 of the Deming cycle). This mechanism is made up of the combination of the FrT with Negative Branch Reservation (NBR).

Let's look at the way it works.

When we bring about the injections, we change our reality. This is very demanding, and makes us go through a series of intermediate states. The changing of states may induce some unwanted effects. In essence, the FrT guides us in the anticipation of these effects and allows us to develop very focused negative branches. As a matter of fact, the FrT and NBR should prevent the occurrence of unwanted effects. The FrT and the associated NBRs are invaluable tools for designing the solution we want and logically controlling its implementation.

Apart from these characteristics, the FrT allows us to identify all the further injections necessary to bring about improvement. This always happens through the interaction of two fundamental logical elements: Necessity and Sufficiency.

In order to achieve an effective change we must have a breakthrough idea. Otherwise, how can we guarantee that the change will not be just more of the same thing? However, in order to get the expected results from the change, we must ensure that everything is in place for the change. We have to check for the sufficiency of the elements.

The other element we have to take into consideration is that knowledge increases continuously.

In order to represent more clearly how we know, learn and undertake the actions necessary to improve our situation, we use a kind of representation that helps us visualize what's happening. We will call this the *knowledge tree*. The knowledge tree assumes that every element is absolutely necessary and every group is sufficient to achieve the higher-level necessary condition.

Every time we learn something new we can add it to the knowledge tree. We do not have to reinvent the wheel every time we want to get a desired outcome. However, there will be dynamic situations that will impose additions, omissions and changes to the basic knowledge tree.

The objective of this book is to show the way to bring about a process of continuous improvement. The knowledge necessary for this process, as we have seen, contains many elements. For this reason we consider it useful to present the development of the knowledge tree step-by-step. In this way we can satisfy two needs, one concerning the completion of our transformation and the other understanding the process we have followed.

- Show the mechanism we use to develop knowledge (necessity and sufficiency essential for bringing about a program of continuous improvement, which is the last step in our Decalogue).
- Make explicit the logic which links the various steps in The Decalogue.

What is the knowledge tree for POOGI?

A necessary condition for embarking on the process of ongoing improvement is the recognition that the performance of any stable system is determined by its constraint(s). Therefore, the acceptance of the concept of the constraint is a necessary condition.

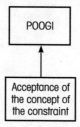

Is it sufficient?

The answer is not surprising. No!

What is missing?

We must know what to do with the constraint. So we add the need for Managing the Constraint, and this is achieved through the Five Focusing Steps (as described in Step Four of The Decalogue).

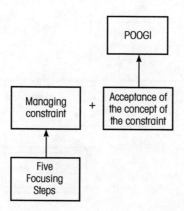

The process of ongoing improvement has three parts. Understanding systems (and making them stable; only a stable system allows the identification of the constraints); managing systems (managing the constraints), and measuring systems (ensuring that we take actions and decisions in the right direction).

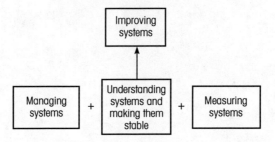

A necessary condition for managing systems is focusing through the Five Focusing Steps. The necessary conditions for measuring systems are the goal of the system, its units of measurement and the operational measurements: T, I, OE (Throughput, Inventory, Operating Expenses). Here is a graph on improving systems.

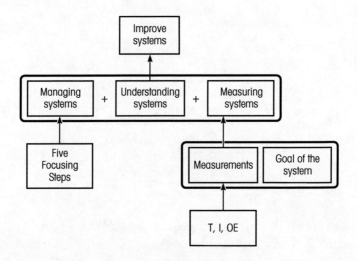

What do we need in order to understand systems?

A system has a goal to achieve. The goal is measured by Throughput (T). Accepting that Throughput is the number one issue is a necessary condition.

What else?

Throughput is achieved through the synchronized efforts of

many resources and disciplines in the organization. This is known as the Throughput chain.

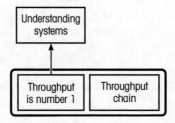

The specific activities performed by each resource are captured in the deployment flow chart which presents us with the necessary understanding of how the system works and achieves its goal.

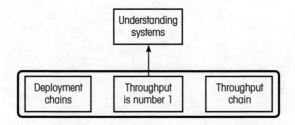

It should be enough for understanding systems, but not enough for managing them. Once such a system has achieved stability in all its basic processes—the heart of Deming's message—then we have to add the part of the TOC knowledge dealing with Managing the Throughput chain. The approach will not be completed if we do not provide the manager with a direction for managing the T-chain. These are the Five Focusing Steps coupled with the three TOC Questions: What to change? What to change to? How to cause the change?

The TP (Thinking Processes) are a set of analytical tools that can help a manager find answers to the three basic TOC questions.

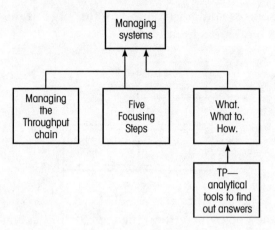

The knowledge tree now takes on the following shape.

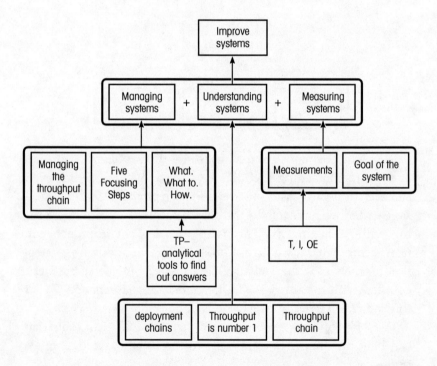

A continuous learning program introduced into an organization must have precise characteristics. This program must involve people directly in a process of learning that encourages them and promotes self-improvement.

The challenge which managers have to face is that they must accept a new role in relation to their staff. They must become teachers, as it is they who must lead the change and nurture the continual growth of the system by means of staff development. In addition, they must learn the tools (and the TOC they spring from), which increase their ability to manage people. Goldratt suggests using this coaching cycle.

1. Pick any problem that bothers you.
2. Identify what type of problem it is.
3. Construct the TP tool that is best to deal with such problems.
4. Find a solution.
5. Prepare the problem for communication.
6. Conduct the communication session.
7. Observe the results.
8. Learn your lessons (and then pick another problem and start again).

A continuous learning process provides management with all the necessary elements for continuously improving the system's performance, and guaranteeing the future of the organization. This gives us the energy and the confidence we need to undertake new actions.

Continuous improvement is assured because the direction to be followed is clear: it's the goal of the system we established at the beginning of our journey.

Chapter 4

The Thinking Processes

The aim of this section is to illustrate briefly the Thinking Processes developed by Eli Goldratt, using some examples.

Indeed, the Thinking Process (TP) tools of Goldratt's Theory of Constraints have been designed with the goal of making people learn better and faster. The tools translate people's intuition into workable knowledge while strengthening the knowledge they already have. Moreover, the TP tools are a very powerful aid in increasing our understanding of our system. When we use these tools we are able to reveal the cause-effect connections that exist in our reality, but which we usually do not see.

The TP tools can be the key to managing the ever-increasing complexity of our environment, be it work or otherwise. More than anything else, we feel that the tools can assist in acquiring that pattern of continuous learning so advocated by both Dr. Goldratt and Dr. Deming.

Core Problem Cloud

The Core Problem Cloud describes the conflict that prevents us from finding a solution to the core problem. There are three major types of core problem clouds.

1. Conflict with the "rules" of the system
2. Personal dilemma of the leader
3. Conflict between functions, management levels or individuals (chronic conflict)

Let's take the first type as an example.

A cloud is a diagram that represents two sides of a conflict with a common goal. Boxes B and D are one side of the conflict; boxes C and D' are the other side of the conflict; box A is the common goal. We read a cloud by inserting the words "in order to" and "must" where we have drawn the arrows.

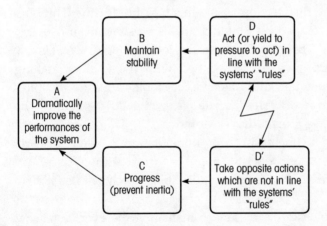

In order to achieve A, **we must** have B;

In order to have B, **we must** have D.

On the other hand,

In order to achieve A, **we must** have C;

In order to have C, **we must** have D'.

The Objective **A** of the cloud is to find a solution to the core problem and to dramatically improve the performance of the system.
The boxes **D** and **D'** of a cloud contain the opposing positions in the conflict. In this case they represent a conflict that the managers have.

D: Act in line with the "rules" of the system—the way they are expected to act by their bosses and the way they are measured by the system.

D': Resist the pressure and take actions that are not in line with the "rules" of the system and actually oppose them.

Box **B** of a cloud contains the *need* that the position **D** is trying to protect, and box **C** contains the *need* box **D'** is trying to protect.

In this case the different actions are driven by these two important business needs. In Box **B** we will find the *necessary condition* of the type of maintaining stability. In order to achieve A (i.e., to dramatically improve the performance of the system), the system must be stable, and the rules help us to get control over the resources, processes and their performances.

In box **C** we may find the *need* for progress and avoiding negative inertia. In order to dramatically improve the performance of the system, we must prevent inertia.

The core problem cloud is sufficient, in many cases, to get consensus on the problem and to start moving. However, in cases of lack of consensus or lack of confidence in the quality of the analysis that has led to the construction of the core problem conflict, there is a need to develop a full CRT—*Current Reality*

Tree—to check the full causalities that lead to the identification of the core problem.

One of the popular ways to construct a CRT is to base it on the Core CRT (CCRT) that is using the core problem cloud.

Current Reality Tree (CrT)

A CrT starts with the identification of Undesirable Effects (UDEs) present in our reality. Such UDEs are not only present, they hurt; they take away some, or much, of the joy that we take in our work. They contribute to form the "prison" created by the way people interact. These UDEs cover a fairly large span; they originate from different sources and have different "weights." Let's choose three of them, possibly very different from each other. For each of them let's build the relevant cloud. **D** will be the UDE and, of course, **D'** will be the corresponding Desirable Effect, DE. Writing **C**, the need which **D'** protects, will probably be easy; **B**, the reason why we put up with **D**, is often a little more tricky to find. Indeed we can always fool ourselves and lie. Unfortunately, inconsistencies will soon be revealed in what follows. The common goal, **A**, is often soon found.

How to construct the clouds for the UDEs? Taking the first of your three UDEs, answer the questions in the following "construction template," in the order indicated. Place your responses in it.

Repeat the same process for the remaining two UDEs that you selected from your UDE list.

Each of the five elements making up each cloud will show a logical overlap, a sort of intersection, a common denominator with the other two. In other words, there will be something in common among the three **A**s, the three **B**s, **C**s, **D**s and **D'**s.

There is a conflict that all of your three UDE clouds are examples of. In order to verbalize this commonality we have to construct the "consolidated cloud." Write the Ds for each of your three clouds. Examine the Ds and write a generic statement

that describes all of them. Each D should be a specific example
of the generic D that you verbalize.

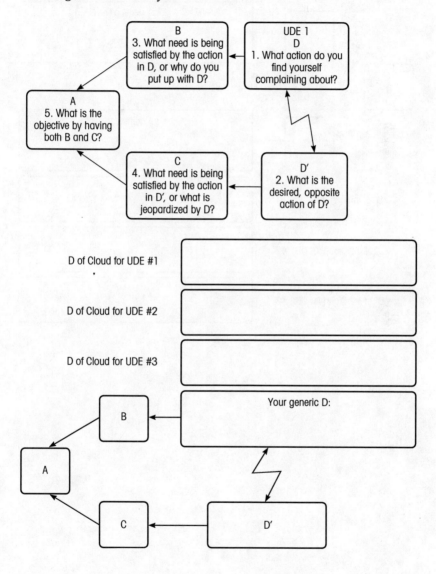

Do the same with D′.

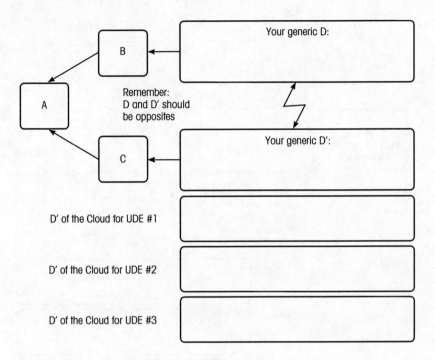

D′ of the Cloud for UDE #1

D′ of the Cloud for UDE #2

D′ of the Cloud for UDE #3

Now do the same with A.

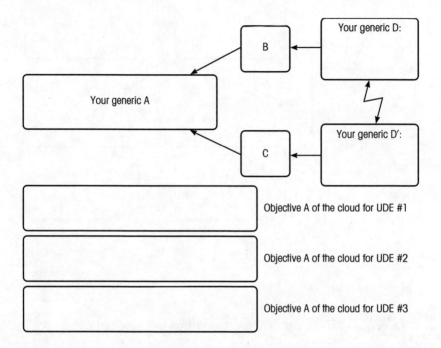

Objective A of the cloud for UDE #1

Objective A of the cloud for UDE #2

Objective A of the cloud for UDE #3

Complete the cloud using the same process for B and C. Check again that each of the boxes in the 3 UDE clouds are specific examples of its corresponding box in the consolidated cloud.

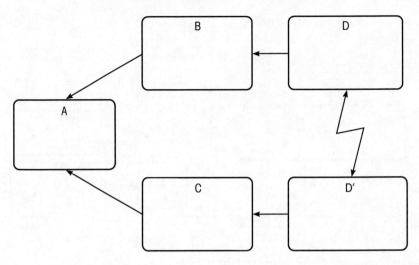

Check the logic of your cloud by reading it the following way:

Horizontal arrows:

"In order to *(have* tip of the arrow), I must *(have* tail of arrow)."

The conflict arrow:
"(D) is in direct conflict with (D')."

Make any changes necessary to make the reading of the cloud flow. The resulting cloud is the Core Problem Cloud.

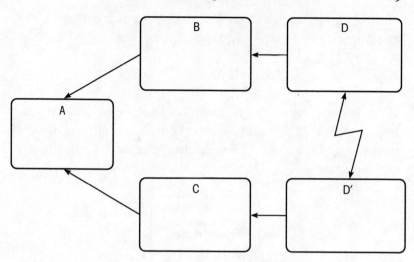

From here, as we saw, we can build the CRT.

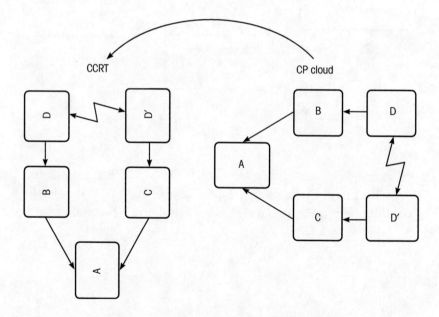

We rotate the CP-Cloud 90 degrees counterclockwise so that the objective **A** is at the bottom of the tree. Then we start to build the causalities upwards adding more sufficiency entities into the causalities. For example, from **A** to **B** and from **A** to **C** and adding more entries into the logic by asking "Why?"

$$A \rightarrow B$$

IF managers want to embark on a Process of Ongoing Improvement **THEN** they must maintain stability **BECAUSE** unstable systems tend to lose Throughput and Throughput is our top priority.

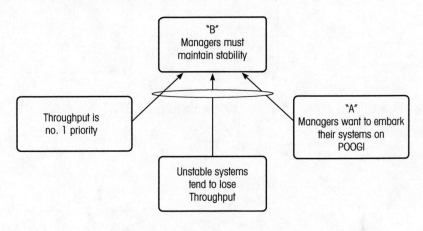

$$A \rightarrow C$$

IF managers want to embark on POOGI, **THEN** they must provide more Throughput **BECAUSE** the only way to sustain continuous growth is through the Throughput channel.

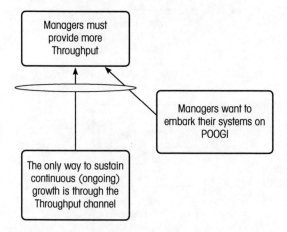

The next step up is **B** → D. *IF* managers must maintain the stability of their systems, *THEN* they must stick to the system's "rules" *BECAUSE* the system's "rules" have been carefully constructed to control people's behavior and performance and controlled people are the best performers.

$$C \rightarrow D'.$$

IF managers must provide more Throughput, *THEN* they must break the system's "rules" *BECAUSE* the system's rules restrict people's initiatives and new Throughput requires new initiatives. (Regular improvement is generated through the learning curve, but it is small compared to the ambitious results managers are expected to produce.)

Now, what happens when we have **D** and **D'** at the same time?

IF managers want to break the "rules" *BUT* they are forced to stick to the "rules," *THEN* they are frustrated, inconsistent and confuse their subordinates. *This leads to* managers losing their credibility in the eyes of their people and losing leadership. All the UDEs, Undesirable Effects of the system, could be connected to this CCRT, especially as a direct consequence of the conflict between **D** and **D'**.

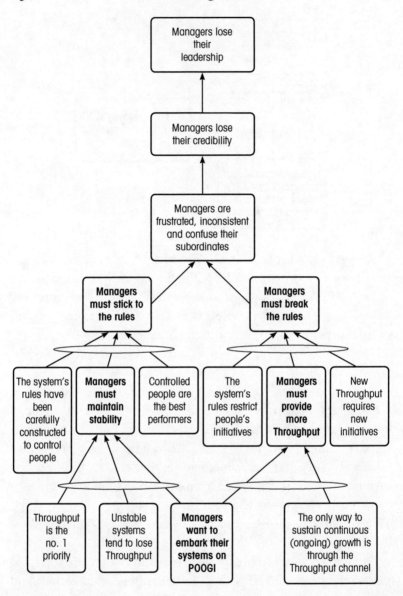

Let's concentrate on the conflict. This is a deep one. Moving from one side of the cloud to the other is painful. Such a conflict, in order to be "evaporated," requires us to surface the assumptions between **D** and **D′**.

"We would like to have **D'** but we have to put up with **D** because . . . ." The becauses are the assumptions; the mental model that forces us to live in this conflict, the profound images that make our reality: they are our limiting factor, they are our constraint. The invalidation of these assumptions shows us the direction of the solution. We give the name "injections" to what invalidates the assumptions. The pursuit of these injections will dictate the priorities; the synchronization needed to achieve the injections will shape the procedures and policies with which we run our organization. The accomplishing of the injections is what operationally moves us toward the goal.

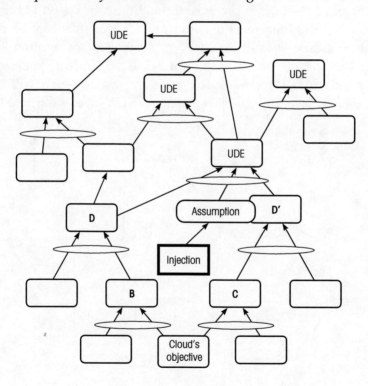

Future Reality Tree

Any set of actions needs to be planned, carried out, and the results studied. This study must provide us with indications on how to improve. This is what Deming called PDSA. TOC provides a tool to design and control the pattern of implementation of the injections found, as well as the means to highlight the need for new ones. The name is *Future Reality Tree* (FRT).

The process of constructing is based on a core FRT that is obtained from the core problem cloud. The starting point (the bottom of the tree) is the breakthrough idea (injection D*) that leads to the achievement of both B and C requirements or needs. Schematically, it is achieved by rotating the core solution 90° clockwise. Later on we add causalities to the structure to ensure we understand the full logic of why the objective will be achieved if we implement the breakthrough idea in our reality.

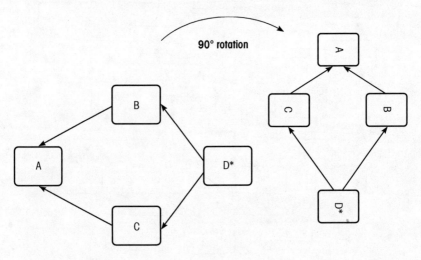

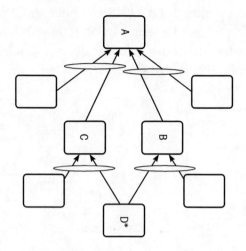

The process can continue until all desired effects (DEs) are logically connected to the FRT. This part, from **A** going up, is called the trunk of the FRT. It reveals how, as a result of the injections found, all of our UDEs will turn into DEs.

At this point the vision of the solution should be clear enough for people to conceptually accept it and move forward.

The FRT is the place where we gather all the supporting logic to "prove" why we claim that the proposed change will bring results.

Injections are what is needed to transform all the UDEs present in our current reality into their opposite, the Desirable Effects of our strongly desired new future reality. FRT puts the Deming cycle into operation. It contains all the elements that guide and sustain continuous improvement. Like the PDSA cycle, FRT is intrinsically systemic and the necessary feedback mechanism, the ACT, is provided by the Negative Branch Reservation.

The bringing about of the injections is extremely demanding; it changes our reality and makes us go through a series of intermediate states. Changing states may induce some unwanted effects. In essence, FRT guides us in the anticipation of these effects, allowing the development of very focused negative branches. As a matter of fact, FRT and NBR should prevent the occurrence of unwanted effects. FRT and the associated NBRs are an invaluable tool in the design of the desired solution and in the logical control of its implementation.

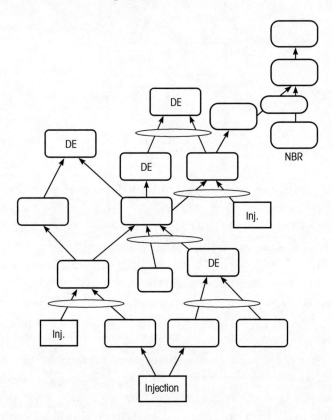

Negative Branch Reservation

This is a Cause and Effect (sufficiency) Tree that starts at the bottom with the new idea—the injection or any part of the solution (FRT)—and develops the logic that states why a negative outcome is unavoidable.

Example: We are in the wilderness and we want to have a cup of tea. Are there NBRs attached to this? We can imagine several, such as: NBR from the fire; NBR with the water we use; the temperature of the tea we drink or what happens if we walk away and do not put the fire out. All of these NBRs have nothing to do with the tea, but they can cause Undesirable Effects on the environment we change.

What can go wrong when we have a fire?

If we are in the woods with a lot of dry leaves and we just start a small fire, without proper care and attention this small fire can become a big fire. The person who raises this reservation, the "Yes, but . . . ," has the knowledge we need in order to construct the NBR, as he has the experience of what can go wrong. We can probe by asking, "How come?"

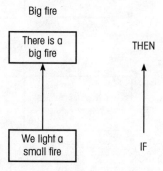

Big fire

IF we light a small fire, THEN there is a big fire BECAUSE: . . . ?

"Because," leads to the answer, "there are dry leaves and a dry wind and therefore the small fire will spread to the leaves and the wind will carry it away rapidly and before you know it you have a big fire you cannot put out as you are not ready for it."

Wow. What a stream of data. But when you actually sort it out, you can see the full logic. This reservation can be captured and presented in a logical way—the NBR.

The NBR may look a little bit over the top to us, but we had better think about the worst scenario rather than handling the situation in a reckless way and suffering the negative consequences. Better safe than sorry.

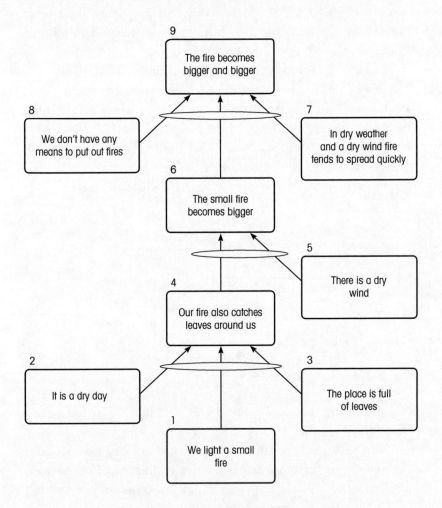

The cup of tea idea—the NBR

So, what do we do with the NBR?

If the logic is explicit enough we can see many ways of "trimming" or removing the negatives, especially by attacking the assumptions entering into the tree from the side. We can examine them and check if we need to take actions to negate their existence or their negative impact.

For example:

Box No. 3 presents an assumption about the reality. The person assumes that there will be many dry leaves around. If they are right, we can agree to clear the area of the fire within a radius of two meters and not to light the fire underneath small trees.

Box No. 5: There may be a dry wind. If this is the case we will look for a protected area that is sheltered from the wind.

Box No. 8: We had not planned to take any means of putting out fires. We can decide to take a fire extinguisher with us, or to check the place for the means available.

Boxes 3, 5 and 8 provide us with the ability to enhance the solution and be more prepared.

Boxes 2 and 7 are facts of life that we can hardly change, but we can adapt our behavior accordingly. If it is too dry and windy, we may decide not to take the risk at all, and drink water, or bring a thermos with hot tea.

Exerting leadership—creating the environment

A leader must create the environment that enables people to give their contribution to the goal of the system.

Such a system, as we saw in Step Three, must be stable in order to be managed. A fundamental reason for wanting to empower people is to create intrinsic stability within the system.

How can we create such an empowered environment? By focusing on two of the most relevant aspects determining instability in an organization:

1. misalignment between authority and responsibility
2. lack of clear instructions

Misalignment Cloud

In a very insightful article, Dr. Goldratt tells of a situation where there is freight to be urgently shipped, but the person responsible for the shipping doesn't have all the necessary information to carry out his duty. An ostensibly simple action could be taken by this person to provide himself with that information and avoid the delay, but there is a company internal procedure that forbids him to do this. This person is in a conflict: take that action (violating the procedure), or do not take that action (delaying the shipment).

The evaporation of this conflict will reveal the importance of redefining the authority of that person and, more generally, the need for systematically providing everybody in an organization with the relevant authority to perform the tasks they are responsible for.

The mechanism that we use to redefine and realign authority and responsibility is the conflict cloud. Frequently, people do not recognize these situations as conflicts, so we often call this cloud the "fire-fighting" cloud. In fact, these clouds are recurrent and often lead to systematic situations of tension in the organization.

Let's say that I am in a situation where if a certain action is not carried out an important need of the system is endangered; and let's also say that I am responsible for that action. As we know, the position of a need in a conflict is **B**.

It may happen that a rule of the system (possibly a company policy and/or procedure) prevents me from fulfilling my responsibility. The place to write this rule is **D'**.

The opposite of this rule is, of course, what would enable the fulfilling of my responsibility, **D**.

The rule of the system that blocks me is originated by another need of the system, **C**. The common goal of the two needs is, obviously, **A**.

The maintenance manager of a medium-size company deals

constantly with the same problem. He is measured on the basis of the machines' downtime, but he does not have the authority of choosing the quality of the spare parts, which currently are purchased solely on the basis of price. The purchasing manager, on the other hand, is measured on the basis of how much he saves on the purchase of spare parts. The maintenance manager drew the following cloud.

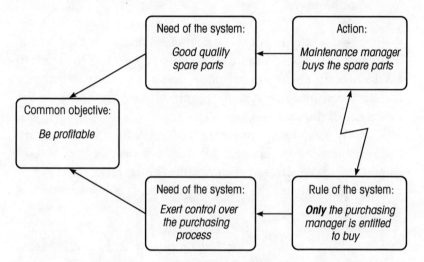

This is a conflict cloud, although constructed in a slightly different way, and it can be evaporated, like any other cloud, by surfacing the assumptions and challenging them.

The injection that evaporates the cloud defines the new authority needed for the person to successfully and straightforwardly carry out his or her tasks.

Assumptions:

1. Only the purchasing manager can strike the best deals.
2. If anybody can buy you lose control of the situation.

Injection:

1. The maintenance manager advises the purchasing manager on the kind of spare parts (and only spare parts) necessary to make the machines work at their best, and
2. The purchasing manager is not measured on the basis of what he saves.

Why is this alignment so important? First, each time somebody who is supposed to do something has to stop his work to ask somebody else's authorization, an unnecessary inefficiency is introduced into our system (graphically this is a loop in the flowchart of the process).

Secondly, each time somebody has to ask for an unnecessary authorization, he or she will feel less responsible/motivated/committed to the successful completion of the task. Thirdly, this mechanism facilitates the discovery of wrong policies/measurements.

Besides misalignment between authority and responsibility, there is also another not less important aspect in empowering people: the ability to communicate clear instructions.

The Transition Tree

The Transition Tree is a tool conceived in order to give clear instructions.

We start realizing that *"as long as we don't know how to verbalize our intuition, the only thing we can delegate is our confusion."* The Transition Tree answers the common questions that we usually ask ourselves when a task is assigned to us.

1. Why are you asking me to do step X?
2. When do I do step X?
3. When do I know I have successfully completed a step so I can move to the next step?

4. What is the objective we're trying to achieve?
5. What is the objective of each step?
6. Why do step X before step Y?
7. How do I know when I have finished?
8. Why do you claim that step X will achieve its purpose?

The Transition Tree contains the following elements:

- The need for the action
- The action itself
- The explanation for why the action will fulfill the need
- The result of the action
- Why the next step is needed

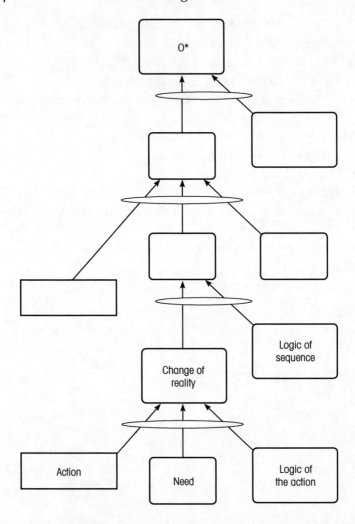

This is the "how to" tree. It shows the detailed logic of how to move from the present into the desired future. The bottom has statements that describe the present state of reality. The top is the goal, the expected change of reality following the conclusion of all the proposed actions.

The creation of a stable system calls for leadership. For Dr. Deming, exercising leadership means giving people pride in their work; freeing them from the chain of wrong interactions;

stimulating their natural, intrinsic motivation to work, and teaching them to learn and be part of a team. The creation of a Deming environment entails the driving out of fear from the workplace, the establishing of open communication among all the levels of the organization and the building of a synchronized mechanism of teamwork. As we saw in Step Two, the tools to enable fear-free communication are the conflict cloud and the NBR.

Sorting out conflicts unleashes energies that have to be conveyed toward the goal. The tool for this purpose is the *Prerequisite Tree*.

The Prerequisite Tree

The Prerequisite Tree allows us to:

- **Break down** a seemingly insurmountable task into its various obstacles. In other words, it highlights the obstacles that come between us and the completion of the task. In this way everyone involved has a clear definition of what makes the task seem insurmountable.
- **Realize** that every obstacle can be overcome by attaching a corresponding intermediate objective, thus giving everyone involved a more consistent strategy.
- **Understand** that correct timing will make it possible to achieve all the objectives and therefore **coordinate** the tactics/actions of everyone involved.

Example: Tea Mission (we want to have a nice cup of tea in the wilderness).

Participants in this ambitious target may raise the following obstacles:

Obstacle 1 We do not have material to burn.

Obstacle 2 Collection of such material is not allowed in the wilderness.

Obstacle 3 There could be a strong wind.

Obstacle 4 We do not have matches.

Obstacle 5 We do not have cups.

Obstacle 6 We don't have a container to boil the water.

   Some of the obstacles are not really difficult to overcome, but we had better not forget them. Actually, we can combine obstacles 4-5-6 into one, such as we always forget to bring everything needed for preparing tea.

Obstacle 1 We do not have material to burn.

Obstacle 2 Collecting of such material in the wilderness is not allowed.

Obstacle 3 There can be a strong wind.

Obstacle 4 We tend to forget to bring everything needed to prepare the tea.

   Obstacle 4 can be overcome by these two Intermediate Objectives (IO):

- We have a packing list for the tea activity.
- The tea kit is loaded into the car.

Both Obstacle 1 and 2 can be overcome by taking some pieces of wood with us in the trunk of the car. In other cases people may suggest that if the objective is to have the tea, we may not actually need to have a fire, but a mobile gas apparatus would do the trick. Creativity is wonderful when you know how to channel it. Obstacle 3 can be overcome by having a sheltered place to light the fire.

   At this point we have a list of three Intermediate Objectives.

IO-1: We have some pieces of wood in the trunk of the car.

IO-3: We have a sheltered place to light the fire

IO-4.1: We have a packing list for the tea activity

IO-4.2: The tea kit is loaded into the car

The last bit is to sort the sequencing of the Intermediate Objectives, in which one has to be in place before the other, and which IOs are not dependent and can be achieved in parallel.

As such, IO-4.1 must be achieved before IO-4.2, otherwise we may prepare and load an incomplete kit into the car.

IO-1 can be achieved in parallel to IO-4.1 and IO-4.2 unless we want to load the pieces of wood last, so that they will be the first to be unloaded from the car. In this case we state that IO-4.1 and IO-1 must be achieved before IO-4.2. IO-3 will be dealt with when we get to the picnic place and therefore is the last one to achieve before we start the process of preparing the tea. Technically one can say that IO-3 is not dependent on the completion of IO-4-2. But, what is the point of searching for a sheltered place if we don't have pieces of wood or the tea kit? We can put it all in a schematic form—the IO map.

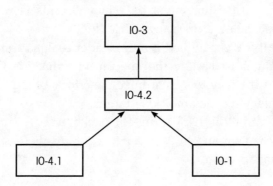

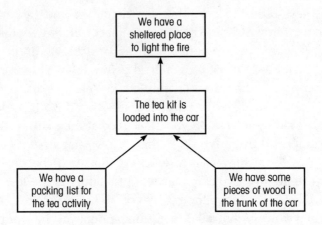

Now we are in the position where we have a map that will help us on the journey of introducing the change into our reality. The IO map draws the logical connections of all the necessary prerequisites that must be achieved. This is why the IO map is also called a *Prerequisite Tree* (PRT).

When all IOs are agreed on, the leader assigns responsibility to individuals to handle the specific Intermediate Objectives. The PRT is the way to synchronize the efforts of the team members in achieving the ambitious target.

The use of PrT and TrT forms the backbone of a synchronized work mechanism and in this respect contains the basic seeds of project management.

Chapter 5

Deming and Goldratt

We do not write stories, we recount lives
PLUTARCH, PARALLEL LIVES

To take great steps we must not only act but also
dream, we must not only plan but also believe
ANATOLE FRANCE

The aim of this section is to provide an outline of the life and work of Dr. W. Edwards Deming and Dr. Eliyahu Moshe Goldratt.

W. Edwards Deming

Dr. Deming was born in Sioux City, Iowa, on October 14, 1900. When he went to Japan for the first time in 1947, he was already a well-known figure in the United States. As a statistician, Deming had already achieved professional and academic results of great relevance. He was a university professor and had a very high profile as a consultant. That year, though, was the turning point of his professional life, and the beginning of a paradigm shift for the management world.

After completing his Ph.D. in physics at Yale in 1927 on the packing effect in helium, Deming spent ten years at the Fixed Nitrogen Research Laboratory at the Department of Agriculture, Washington, D. C.

In 1939 he joined the National Bureau of the Census, Washington, D. C. as Head Mathematician and Adviser in Sampling. The work he developed with the census operations brought him international fame and led to his initial visit to Japan.

In 1925, while doing work at the Western Electric Hawthorne plant, Chicago, Deming met Walter Shewhart. Without any doubt, the most important influence on Deming's thinking came from their lifelong collaboration and friendship.

Shewhart, a physicist from Bell Labs, had studied the variation in the measured qualities of parts and products produced for the Bell System. The need for reducing this variation, thus improving the quality, led him to the development of the control chart as early as 1924. In 1931 Shewhart published his famous book, *Economic Control of Quality of Manufactured Product* (Van Nostrand Company, Inc.), where he investigates the nature of control and its application to the improvement of quality, laying the foundations for the theory of variation.

In 1936, Deming invited Shewhart to give four lectures at the Graduate School in the Department of Agriculture. Those lectures, edited by Deming, were subsequently published by the same department under the title: *Statistical Method from the Viewpoint of Quality Control* (Washington, 1939).

During World War II, Deming and Shewhart worked together, by invitation of the War Department, to improve the quality of the production of weapons via the use of statistical methods. His work for the war effort brought Deming nationwide fame, and Stanford University, following his suggestion, instituted a ten-day course in statistical quality control. Deming took part in the first 23 of these courses, which helped American war industries develop quality control.

In 1946 Deming became a professor at the Graduate School of Business, New York University, and a year later was invited to Japan by General MacArthur to work with his economic and scientific staff. There, he was involved in the survey of housing, agriculture, fishing, industry and the population census. Most importantly, he began his interaction with Japanese statisticians and scientists.

In 1950 Dr. Deming was invited by the Japanese Union of Scientists and Engineers (JUSE) to return to Japan to teach methods for the achievement of Quality.

"The Control Chart Is No Substitute For The Brain" is what Dr. Deming suggested his audience write in their notebooks (in capital letters) on July 10, 1950, the first day of his first lecture in Japan.(12) Why is it important to recall this? Because many people think that the essence of what Deming taught the Japanese in those days was statistics.

We can see this is not true from Deming's diary entry for the first day of his eight-day course to 230 engineers jam-packed into the auditorium of the Japan Medical Association in Ochanomizu: "Professor Masuyama and assistants will teach the statistical control of quality in the afternoon. I shall teach during the forenoons the theory of a system, and cooperation."(13)

The control chart is a very simple technique—even assistants can teach it. What is important is the knowledge that we can derive from it, Deming called that knowledge *profound.*

Not long after, Ichiro Ishikawa, as representative of the industrialists, invited Deming for a series of meetings to ask him what the obligations and duties of top managers were. At the end of those meetings, Ishikawa sent telegrams to the top 21 industrialists in the country to invite them to a meeting to be held at the Industry Club, Tokyo. Deming met every single top manager in the country in 28 ensuing meetings, which started in January 1951.

In 1974 an American industrialist heard Deming's name mentioned in particularly meaningful circumstances. William Conway was president of the Nashua Corporation at the time. Nashua, in a consortium of five companies, including the Japanese company Ricoh, was currently involved in the development of a revolutionary copying system. As the product was to be manufactured in Japan, many of the high level technical meetings were held in Tokyo. On his return from one of these meetings, the head of Research and Development gave Conway a strange report on what had happened. Instead of being re-

ceived with the traditional Japanese courtesy, the Nashua delegation had been almost completely ignored and the few meetings which were actually held took place at strange times. When
Conway asked for an explanation the manager replied:

"They're all nuts over there. They're all collecting data on
stuff, plotting them on all these little charts, and then they're all
going round fixing everything. . . . Everyone's doing it—the
president, the vice president of sales, the controller, the R&D
chemists, the hourly workers, the foremen, the accountants. Everybody is doing it, Bill—they're all doing it!"

What was going on? What were they all doing?

The Ricoh company had undertaken a demanding five-year
program to obtain the most prestigious Japanese industrial
award. The Nashua delegation had had the misfortune to arrive
at the company a few days before the deadline for the admission
of Ricoh for the Deming Prize.

When near the end of the 70s Conway, who in the meantime
had become CEO of Nashua, found himself competing with the
Japanese, it was clear that the problem was not just lower costs
but a higher quality and more reliable product. During his visits
to Japan Conway paid increasing attention to Deming's name
and discovered the importance and respect the Japanese attributed to Deming. Nonetheless, nothing happened until 1979.

On Tuesday, March 6, 1979, Conway phoned Deming at his
Washington home, and asked him for an appointment. It was
the first time the managing director of a large American firm
had contacted Deming directly. Deming went to see Conway
that Friday. The story he had to tell bordered on the absurd.
When Conway asked Deming to be a consultant for Nashua, he
accepted on one condition: that Conway himself, as CEO, would
lead the change in the company. American managers had
proved disappointing in the past. Conway's acceptance was the
starting point for what Professor Henry Neave, the source of
this episode, calls Deming's "Western Renaissance."

What Dr. Deming *really* taught the Japanese was the interpretation of the control chart and the fundamental management thinking that interpretation has to inspire.

By the end of the 70s, the world knew that they had listened. But up until 1980, Deming lived a paradox. In Japan he was revered as the man who had contributed so enormously to the renaissance of the economy, yet in the United States he was largely ignored.

After the war, Uncle Sam had no competitors in the marketplace; managers found Deming's severe and often abrasive words extravagant, extreme, or, to say the least, unnecessary.

The United States was the only country that did not need to rebuild its industrial system. Effectively America's success in the 50s and 60s was not due to excellence in manufacturing and service but to the fact that they were the only ones who could produce and sell anything at all. In Deming's words:

"They were in a crisis—they knew that. We're in a crisis and do not know it. Our crisis is more severe. They knew it. All they had to do was look out the window. We're in a worse crisis because people do not know it. They think because they had breakfast this morning everything is all right."(14)

By 1980 the American GNP per capita had fallen from first to seventh place in the world. Something was going wrong inside the American giant. The NBC White Paper entitled *If Japan Can . . . Why Can't We?* helped people to understand the challenge that U.S. industry was facing. That documentary, broadcast June 24, 1980, was aimed at explaining the factors that enable a nation to continually increase its productivity, quality and competitive position, as well as the consequences of failing to do so. It explained, as never before, the reasons for the Japanese success. *If Japan Can . . . Why Can't We?* was watched by 14 million people that night, and later became NBC's most requested program of all time, with thousands of requests for videotapes and transcripts.

One of the reasons for this success was the featuring in that video of an old gentleman with a deep, thundering voice, uttering words of unprecedented power and relevance: Dr. W. Edwards Deming.

Dr. Deming died December 20, 1993. What happened in the 13 years following the NBC program takes up a relevant part of the management literature in the Western world. As William Conway said, "Deming is the father of the third wave of the industrial revolution."

The major channel for disseminating Deming's management philosophy during his lifetime was the legendary "four-day seminar," in which Deming lectured to groups of hundreds of top executives all around the world. He taught at least ten seminars per year between 1980 and 1993, reaching over 200,000 managers. Almost every top manager in the United States, from GM to Ford, from AT&T to Xerox, to name a few, was exposed to Deming's teachings in those years. Fifteen universities granted him *Honoris Causa* degrees. In 1985 he became Distinguished Lecturer in Management at Columbia University. In 1982 the MIT Center for Advanced Engineering Studies published *Out of the Crisis*. In 1993 it published *The New Economics for Industry, Government, Education,* where Deming presents his legacy to the world—the Theory of Profound Knowledge.

Dr. Deming received the Shewhart Medal in 1955 from the American Society for Quality Control. In 1960, he became the first American to receive the Second Order Medal of the Sacred Treasure from the Emperor of Japan. This was for the contribution his work had made to the improvement in the Japanese economy and exports. In 1986 Deming was inducted into the Science and Technology Hall of Fame in Dayton, Ohio.

In 1987, Deming became Honorary Life President of the BDA, the British Deming Association, Salisbury, U.K., a not-for-profit organization with the goal of spreading awareness of the Deming management philosophy. In the same year, he received the National Medal of Technology from President Ronald Reagan at the White House.

When Deming died, obituaries were published in all the major newspapers in America, Japan and Europe. In one of them, the writer reported Deming's reply to the question of how he would like to be remembered in his native land:

"Well, maybe . . . as someone who spent his life trying to keep America from committing suicide."(15)

Deming lived a long and extraordinarily intense life, a life in which he never ceased to learn. The attempt to present his teachings is anything but an easy task. In 65 years of academic and professional activity, Deming wrote seven books and more than 170 other publications, undertaking teaching and consulting activity in the America, Japan and many other countries all over the world. (A very comprehensive account of his message can be found in *The Deming Dimension*, SPC Press, Knoxville, Tennessee, by Professor Henry Neave.)

In the continuum of his activity we can identify the following three phases:

1. What he learned from Shewhart and his work until 1950
2. The message to Japanese management
3. Following the NBC documentary, his work in the U.S.— *The Theory of Profound Knowledge*

Throughout his life Deming never stopped acknowledging the work of Walter Shewhart as a primary source of his learning.

One can say that the content of my seminars . . . and the content of my books . . . are based in large part on my understanding of Dr. Shewhart's teaching. Even if only ten percent of the listeners absorb part of Dr. Shewhart's teachings, the number may in time bring about change in the style of Western management.

—W. EDWARDS DEMING(16)

As was mentioned earlier, the problem that Shewhart had to face was one of lack of uniformity in the production of components and products for the telephone industry. In essence, his effort was aimed at finding a method to reduce the excessive variability in the production of these components. The result of his work was the theory of statistical control of a process, and the devising of the control charting technique.

Shewhart realized that a process can be affected by two kinds of variation.

1. Variation from repetitive causes, i.e., from hour to hour, from batch to batch, from operator to operator. He named these causes, which are intrinsic to the process, *chance causes* (Deming called them *common causes*).
2. Variation originated by an event that is in some way external, not intrinsic to the process; a variation that is *assignable* to some specific event. (Deming named these causes *special causes*.)

In coping with these two types of variation while trying to achieve uniformity, one falls into two types of error.

Error 1. Considering the outcome of a process attributable to a special cause of variation, when instead it came from common causes.

Error 2. Considering the outcome of a process attributable to common causes of variation when instead it came from a special cause.

Both these errors are costly and, unfortunately, unavoidable. Any attempt to **always** attribute any outcome to one of the two causes will result in maximizing the loss due to the other. (The failure to recognize the difference between the two types of variation leads to actions taken on the process that result in worsening its performance. Deming defined this as *tampering*.)

In his quest for uniformity Shewhart decided to proceed in the following way: Make both Error 1 and Error 2 now and then, but regulate the frequencies of the two errors in order to minimize the economic loss from the combination of the two.

This is the conceptual backbone of the control chart with the 3-sigma limits. Control limits are, in every respect, action limits; they tell you when it is worth taking action on a process. Control limits provide the indications for hunting down the causes for excessive variation; they allow the making of rational decisions that enable the process to be brought into a stable state, a state of statistical control.

Why is a state of statistical control desirable?

Because only in such a state can we aim at a predictable state of uniformity; only in this state can we predict the future outcome of a process; only in this state can we begin to plan our action for the improvement of quality and productivity. We need a state of control in order to predict. The essence of Statistical Process Control, SPC, is prediction.

In the foreword to the 1986 reprinting of *Statistical Method from the Viewpoint of Quality Control*, Deming wrote:

"Another half-century may pass before the full spectrum of Dr. Shewhart's contribution has been revealed in liberal education, science and industry."

Deming was certainly Shewhart's best student; his life was a crusade to make the world aware of the magnitude of the implications of this message. But because the United States was unaware of impending crisis, he began that crusade in Japan.

The message to Japanese management

Let's say it one more time: Deming did not teach the Japanese statistical process control. He taught them how to interpret control charts; he taught them their implications. Deming taught Japanese industrialists and engineers what it takes to build a country following the profound knowledge that only Shewhart's theory of variation can provide. We can summarize Deming's teachings in Japan briefly as follows.

1. Production must be seen as a system encompassing customers and suppliers. The customer is the most important part of the production line; without the customer there is no production line. The suppliers are partners, and companies must work together with their suppliers for the continuous improvement of the quality of incom-

ing materials and reduction of variation. The relationship between customer and supplier must be win-win.

2. Quality is made in the boardroom, right at the top. The quality of what a company produces can only be as good as the quality of the managerial actions taken by the top managers. The reasons for poor results have to be found in the decisions made by the managers. Never blame the workers.

3. Improving a process triggers a chain reaction. If we improve quality, costs will diminish, productivity will improve, we will manage to conquer the market thanks to higher-quality lower-price products, and we will create wealth for ourselves and also for others by always creating more work.

4. Continuous learning and continuous improvement, as we have seen, follow the Shewhart cycle: Plan - Do - Check - Act (Deming replaced c = check with s = study, making it PDSA).

5. Need for trust and cooperation between companies. Anything new learned in one company must be taught to all other companies, including competitors.

The need to work as a system and to cooperate was understood immediately by Japanese managers. These concepts form the basis for the Deming Prize, awarded every year since 1951 to companies that have attained commendable results in the practice of statistical process control, and to individuals who have carried out excellent research in the theory or application of statistical process control.

Deming explained these concepts in the NBC documentary *If Japan Can . . . Why Can't We?*(17) After that broadcast, he became increasingly more popular in the United States and the Western world. In the remaining part of his life Dr. Deming wrote his two most famous books, *Out of the Crisis* (1986) and *The New Economics* (1992). Deming's goal was clear: the transformation of the Western style of management.

The Theory of Profound Knowledge
(or System of Profound Knowledge)

> *The 14 points for management in industry, education*
> *and government follow naturally as application of this*
> *outside knowledge [Profound Knowledge], for transfor-*
> *mation from the present style of Western management*
> *to one of optimization.*
>
> —W. Edwards Deming

It is very common, and, sadly, very wrong, to hear comments on Deming's work that sound like "It's SPC," or "It's about the 14 points." Others think about it as team and teamwork. Some think of it as some sort of humanitarian stuff. The one that upset Deming the most was "It's about TQM," referring to Total Quality Management. He did not want his name to be associated with TQM, as aware as he was of the risk of "guilt by association."

For Deming, quality management means a commitment to the continuous improvement and innovation of products and processes. To achieve this, it is mandatory to build the organization as a clear and shared system in which interpersonal relations are not of dependence but interdependence, where communication is encouraged, and where the needs of the individual are catered to and combined with group work.

An organization determined to build Quality helps its people to understand the systemic nature of their work. It encourages the study of effects in order to discover their profound causes, and orients itself to looking at processes instead of just concentrating on results.

Deming's vision of Quality entails a radical re-thinking of company management; it requires a purely intercultural approach, and the study of areas of knowledge that are very different from each other. Deming's work is generally referred to as *"Deming's Philosophy."* Its bases are contained in the Theory of

Profound Knowledge (TPK), or, in his own words, "knowledge for leadership of transformation." They are:

1. Appreciation for a system
2. Knowledge about variation
3. Theory of knowledge
4. Psychology of individuals, society, and change

The application of TPK transforms the present style of Western management to one of optimization. The various elements of TPK cannot be separated; they interact with each other.

1. For Deming, an organization is a system. What is a system? A network of interdependent components that work together to try to accomplish the aim of the system. Without an aim there is no system.
2. Statistics (or theory of variation) will allow us to understand whether our production processes are stable (in statistical control), and what their intrinsic capacity is to supply the output required. Moreover, the understanding that variability is a phenomenon common to all human activities provides us with a conceptual basis for the correct management of staff performance and the improvement of process capacity.
3. Regarding the theory of knowledge, management involves predicting and anticipating what will happen if certain actions are taken. For Deming, knowledge is prediction. A theory of knowledge explains how the combination of methods, people, environment and equipment produces a foreseen change. Knowing the system means anticipating the implications that actions taken will have on the system itself in its entirety. Knowledge can only come from theory. Information is not knowledge.
4. Psychology helps us to understand people and their behavior and to appreciate their natural inclination toward learning and being innovative. The psychological aspect

of the Deming approach to human resource management is radically different from current practice in Western companies. For Deming, staff performance must be managed and not evaluated *a posteriori*. Moreover, the malfunctioning of an organization is almost entirely due to the misunderstanding of the system by the management.

TPK is what Deming taught in the United States and Western world organizations. Quality management is for Dr. Deming the application of these principles to the management of organizations.

The work of Dr. Deming provides an exceptionally comprehensive framework for continuous improvement and draws from ever-evolving bodies of knowledge. Indeed, the might of his achievements has deeply influenced the ideas presented in this book.

None of the authors had the privilege to talk to and learn directly from Dr. Deming. We do not claim that Deming would have agreed in full with what we have presented. What we feel was the major input from Deming is his intellectual courage, his zest for learning, his unending quest for knowledge. We feel that the methodology that we present here is the offspring of his vision for "a better way."

Eliyahu M. Goldratt

Dr. Eliyahu (Eli) Moshe Goldratt is the creator of TOC, the Theory of Constraints. Since 1975 he has continuously pursued the rules, concepts and tools for a real process of ongoing improvement.

He started his journey by constructing a scheduling software for production environment that was called OPT—Optimized Production Technology. This software was based on a breakthrough solution that he had developed for his Ph.D. thesis. He built a company to promote this software, first in Israel and later in the United States and Europe.

The desire to find the process of ongoing improvement led Dr. Goldratt to challenge every single step in the development of his company and the ability of his ideas to bring people to embark on such a process.

The outcome of the continuous analysis brought him to embark on new areas and new initiatives and to cross uncharted waters.

Goldratt's most famous publication is his book *The Goal*, which he wrote in 1984 as a "marketing brochure" to promote his solution for production management. The book can be described as a departure from the conventional way of writing a textbook. It is presented as a novel, using present tense and first person. Yet, the story of Alex Rogo, the plant manager who struggles to save his and his people's jobs, has been widely accepted by managers all over the world. Over two million books have been sold in America and hundreds of thousands more sold throughout the rest of the world. *The Goal* has been translated into over twenty-five languages. Goldratt's books are welcomed not only in developed countries but also in India, China, South America, and Central Europe, not to mention Israel, the country where a person has difficulty being a prophet in his own homeland.

What is so unique about *The Goal?*

The first and the strongest element is the way it affects its readers. Managers feel that the author has secretly visited their plant, that he has been talking about their situation, their problems and in many cases about their own people. Everyone can easily identify with Alex, with Bill Peach as his boss, Bucky Burnside as a customer, Bob Donovan as a production manager, and in many cases, Julie as a wife who is a little bit unhappy with her workaholic husband.

Goldratt discovered that the first step in getting buy-in is to get agreement on the problem that we need to address. He achieved this through listening to people's complaining and moaning about things that do not go the way they would like them to. He called these problems "undesirable effects"—UDEs.

Chapter One of *The Goal* is the day-to-day reality of many production managers at all levels from all over the world. The book
deals with their problems, using their language, their terminol-
ogy, and unleashes their intuition. Dr. Goldratt believes in people's intuition. He claims that intuition does not come from thin
air—it stems from experience accumulated over the years. It is
in many cases non-verbalized knowledge that people have, the
existence and importance of which they are unaware. This intuition is a major element in the buy-in of the problem, understanding the solution and the ability to implement the suggested
change in reality to get better performance.

Getting agreement on the problem is critical, but it is only the
first step in the journey that the reader goes through in *The Goal.*
The solution that is developed is simple, practical and makes a
lot of sense, even to people who are outside manufacturing industries.

In early 1987 a small American company reported in *Inc* magazine that through the reading of *The Goal,* company leaders
managed in 12 months to dramatically improve their operational performance and to impact the bottom line of the company.(18) Goldratt was puzzled. How come an investment as
small as purchasing 20 copies of *The Goal* secured more benefits
than a big investment in expensive consulting services or costly
software? At the same time, this short story gave him the direction for a missing element he was longing to find in his journey.

Four years earlier, at the beginning of 1983, in a meeting of
top management of his worldwide organization (Creative Output), Goldratt had started to actively search for the Process of
Ongoing Improvement (or POOGI). Creative Output was a company that had an advanced scheduling software called OPT—
Optimized Production Technology. It was a mature product that
was developed in 1975 and had been implemented in over 200
companies with considerable success.

The software, accompanied by strong implementation teams,
gave a new meaning to scheduling. Schedules were not just production timetables. They contained three features. They were

realistic (finite capacity); they ensured financial benefits (through the completion of orders in time), and they were immune to disruptions (capable of handling "Murphies").

The reality of production environments in the late 1970s was bottlenecks—the big and expensive machines that blocked production. Goldratt's software, OPT, was capable of handling bottlenecks. It helped to identify the constraining resources, to schedule them to their maximum potential, and to ensure that material was released on time.

Everything had been fine from 1975 to 1982. Creative Output (CO) had grown nicely. After several successful implementations in Israel, Goldratt and his partners opened a company in the United States called CO Inc. in 1979, and a British subsidiary in 1982. The company was number six in the *Inc.* magazine rating for growth, and in 1983 it had over 250 employees worldwide.

But 1982 was a tough year as recession hit the aerospace industry, due to cuts in the space programs, and the automotive industry started to feel the competition from Japan. Recession means a slow-down in manufacturing and this caused reduction in demand, leading to the disappearance of bottlenecks.

The recession started to impact Creative Output as well. Even though the company was doing well, the image of "bottleneck busters" caused difficulties in marketing and selling the software and its implementations.

Goldratt, the chairman of the company and the driving force behind its development, investigated the situation. It was apparent that the Japanese won the competition due to better response to the market, and their low inventory was a key competitive edge. The software, and Goldratt's knowledge, were good and quick answers to the Japanese threat. So, why was it so difficult to persuade companies to acquire the software?

So Goldratt started by analyzing the performance and behavior of existing clients. As on-time shipping was achieved regularly, the analysis was done in the area where they were definitely lagging behind the Japanese—inventory. Special attention was paid to the time-related part of inventory, WIP, Work In Progress, or Work In Process, depending on which country you are in.

The pattern that was revealed was interesting (to use British understatement). In the first six months of a typical implementation of the scheduling package, in the pilot area WIP dropped to at least 50% of the value it had at the beginning of the study. However, the rate of inventory reduction started to slow down dramatically in the following period of 6 to 12 months, and in several cases some deterioration in the achievements was detected. The results were presented on this graph.

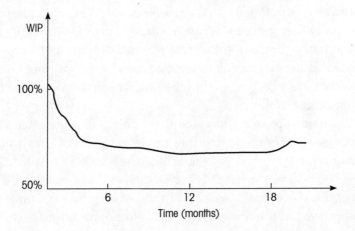

Actually, this pattern was not that bad. Most companies perceived that a reduction of 30 to 50% in inventory was more than needed in order to keep their headquarters happy. But Eli was not happy. He already knew that the Japanese were doing better, and that they had their own continuous improvement process, which worked but was too slow.

It was obvious to Goldratt that he was on the right track, but something prevented the companies from continuing to strive for more improvements. He knew that the software could do it, but most companies did not use the software correctly and therefore did not get what they could out of it.

The thing that blocked further improvements was neither the bottleneck nor any other capacity constraint resource. It was a new type of constraint—measurement and policies. This was discovered through the realization that the slowdown in the inventory reduction happened after the six-month pilot period. This occurred when the implementation teams of Creative Output left the premises and the schedules were produced and controlled by the local teams. They were technically capable, but they had to fight with their own management and with the measurement systems that punished them for following the schedules.

So the solution to the problem was to change the strategy of Creative Output. Rather than selling software, the company moved to key projects which included software, training and consultancy. Besides software implementations these projects contained heavy training of top and middle management in the concepts of scheduling and in the production solution known as Drum-Buffer-Rope.

The new approach addressed the problem to some extent, and facilitated better understanding in Goldratt's people as well as the new customers. However, selling the idea was as difficult as before, and even more difficult as the price tag went up. Even when they eventually agreed to the project, the high price did not prevent top management from tampering with the schedules.

A year later, in 1984, Goldratt wrote *The Goal*. It was an attempt to promote the knowledge in a way that would make it easy for newcomers to take his ideas on board. The book was written using the "Socratic Approach." Coming from an academic background, Goldratt promised himself that he would not participate in the race of professors writing textbooks to torture their students. Therefore, he disguised the book in the form of a novel. Even though the book has been a remarkable success, the marketing constraint was not overcome.

During the New Year break of 1986, Goldratt and his team dealt with the issue of defining the goal of Creative Output. It became clear that the quest for continuous improvement bumped into a slight resistance. The discussion brought up a clear definition of the goal of the company. To make money while bringing wealth to its customers, and using the latest knowledge.

For a company that makes money through selling software and consultancy it was quite a blow. Within a few months the company split up into two camps that were drifting apart. One part supported Goldratt in the quest for bringing benefits to the clients, while the majority wanted to keep on just selling the software. The main argument of the opposition was that the buyers are grown-ups and that they have to take responsibility for their own actions. Therefore, if they buy excellent software, it was their own duty to use it properly and get the benefits.

Goldratt's approach was that there is more that the provider can do in order to ensure that the customers get their benefits. He assumed that the marketing constraint is not in the market, but inside the company. Product offering, company policies and the attitude of salespeople can dramatically reduce the ability to sell. Therefore, he wanted the team to keep on searching for better ways to influence the customers to properly use the ideas. The forced change in policy was unavoidable. No more consultancy. No more software.

This policy was dictated based on the realization that neither software nor consultancy is the answer for ongoing improvement. He knew that there was something missing. He called it "Thoughtware," but it was in its infancy and most people were confused about what it was.

Within a couple of months he found himself out of the company. His partners, who had the majority of shares, called a special board meeting, and in August 1986 he was removed from his position as chairman of the company that he had established ten years earlier. Goldratt left Creative Output with a small group of supporters and started all over again.

In October 1986 he established the Avraham Y. Goldratt Institute (AGI), a U.S. partnership with headquarters in New Haven,

Connecticut. This part of the story is not gossip. It is the story of his commitment to his goal and to the vision of how a "super consultant" should behave. This commitment cost him his company and a loss of many millions of dollars. The new organization was committed to the development of the missing element of ongoing improvement—education.

While setting up the new organization, Goldratt constructed an innovative structure to support its unique goal, which is to generate and disseminate knowledge.

The organizational structure of AGI is a partnership created to bring Goldratt's ideas to the marketplace. Goldratt's approach acquired a new name—TOC (the Theory Of Constraints).

The first ten years of the Goldratt Institute were devoted to the development of TOC, its concepts, educational products and conceptual tools. TOC is defined as the ability to construct and communicate common sense solutions. The main educational program developed by the Institute is called the *Jonah Program*. Goldratt chose the name Jonah for his visionary "super consultant." A Jonah is a person who has a powerful set of logical tools—Thinking Processes (TP)—enabling him/her to help people who want to help themselves. A Jonah is an educated person who teaches, consults, coaches and mentors his students, guiding them to develop and implement their own solutions so that they can embark on ongoing improvement.

The first Jonah Program took place in the summer of 1987, and since then thousands of top executives have graduated in programs all over the world. In their companies Jonahs are either the leaders with the vision who take their companies on this path, or the facilitators who help other managers to develop their own solutions and implement them.

In order to "build" a Jonah, Goldratt had to address a major dilemma that constrained managers who considered embarking on a process of continuous improvement. All managers who want to succeed in their jobs must fulfill two major requirements. They must achieve the commitments for the short term (budget or any top management initiative) and at the same time get the support of their people and enhance their capabilities to respond to ever-increasing challenges.

These two requirements are not negotiable, but seem to be in conflict.

The conflict is caused by the different modes of operations that are required from the managers. The first requirement demands short term, quick fix and imposed actions. The second requirement demands involving people, education, training and empowerment. These are two fundamentally different managerial styles, autocratic versus a more democratic style.

The autocratic, brute force corporate approach has its own merits, but in many cases it has a major deficiency. After the quick fix there is a danger of stagnation and maybe even deterioration in performance. A typical performance curve under the quick fix reign looks like this:

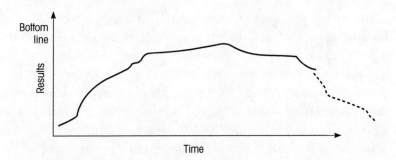

By contrast, the opposite is a knowledge-based consensus approach. It takes more time at the beginning, as there is a need to do homework. This is in order to find the right problem, to devise simple and practical solutions and to get the buy-in from the people whose collaboration is required. Later on, the investment in the team and the common language pays off, as the team is capable of addressing future challenges with better success.

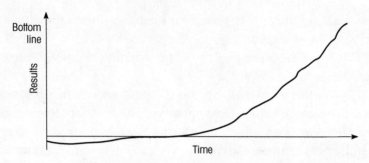

The solution to the dilemma comes through the transfer of the Jonah knowledge to two key individuals—the team leader, who sets the direction and supports the process, and a facilitator for the team and for the individuals. For that, Goldratt had to develop the Thinking Processes—the tools to carry out the methodological process to develop and implement common sense solutions.

All in all, the development of the Thinking Processes was lengthy and painful. Goldratt wanted to bring science to management. In his eyes, managing people and organizations should not be a "soft science," it should be a "hard science" like physics, chemistry and biology. In his view every science had gone through three distinct stages: classification, correlation and Effect-Cause-Effect. While the hard sciences are already in the third stage the soft sciences—dealing with people—are in the correlation stage.

Management is about prediction. A manager is expected to make a decision and to take actions in accordance with that decision. Therefore, it is crucial that a manager is capable of predicting the outcome of his actions. In order to predict, managers should be equipped with knowledge. Therefore, management has to move to the third stage of science: *Effect-Cause-Effect*.

Effect-cause-effect is the process by which science proceeds in investigation, in finding speculative causes for an existing phenomenon. Therefore it covers two steps. In the first step we check the effect and develop a cause and effect relationship to build a hypothesis for what the reason for the existence of the effect is. In the second step we verify the validity of this causality by checking that another effect that stems from the same cause exists as well.

The last three paragraphs demonstrate some of the difficulties with Dr. Goldratt's theories. Even though he really tried to make them simple, they still seem complicated and cumbersome to many people. The introduction of scientific thinking to management has not been easy. As management is taught as a soft science and as many managers were promoted into their positions without proper training and education, conceptual thinking and systems thinking are not their major strength.

But the remedy to this obstacle is the creation of a new language to facilitate the process of ongoing improvement. The first language Goldratt developed was based on a scientific approach. As he has a Ph.D. in physics, his first attempt was to bring the language of physics to management. Only a tiny fraction of the people who were exposed to it could understand it well enough to use it to solve their own problems. (Part of the scientific way of thinking is described in Goldratt's book *What is This Thing Called TOC?*). The scientific thinking methods were not adopted, but the structural framework was created. These are: the logical cause and effect "Trees" to record knowledge, and the "Clouds" to capture problems and to create brainstorming situations that can lead to the invention of breakthrough ideas.

Once the logical structures were in existence, the question was how to transfer the knowledge to others. There was a need for clear instructions, but they were not good enough. The major measurement for good, logical work is that people who come across it state that "It is just common sense." Common sense is the highest appraisal one can give to an argument, but it is not that easy to find the rules of writing and communicating common sense.

In 1991, after yet another deep analysis of the situation, Dr. Goldratt changed the direction of the development. This time he based the Thinking Processes on "good old intuition." Intuition is the thing that tells us when something is right or not; it tells us when things make sense to us or not; it guides us when we have to react instinctively.

The move to intuitively-based thinking processes made a significant impact on the development of TOC and the ability to bring it to many people. From the end of 1991 to 1996 a set of logical tools was developed and tested in a multitude of places and industries. The good news is that the young generation can take it easily on board. In May 1998 the Chief Inspector of Education of the British Government visited a nursery and infant school in Nottingham. The BBC interviewed young children of five and six years old and they told the reporter how they use the "Cloud" to solve their problems and disputes. High schools in Detroit, Michigan, reported on the successful use of TOC "Management Skills" in peer mediation. The not-so-good news is that many "oldies" struggle to take it on board.

The Thinking Processes have been used in developing applications for specific areas and subjects. The most famous area of Goldratt's application is production and logistics. In this area Goldratt invented breakthrough ideas that have been proven to work again and again. The recognition of the constraint as the one single element that determines the Throughput of a system is Goldratt's major contribution. "Constraint Management" is known in the USA as one of the leading methods for production and logistics. It also has been acknowledged by QS9000 (the quality standards for the big automotive companies) and will be acknowledged by the new revisions of ISO9000.

Besides production, Goldratt developed breakthrough ideas in distribution, project management, sales and marketing, supply chain, measurements and day-to-day problems.

In mid-1996 he announced that the development of the basic tools and methodology had reached a "good enough" stage and that the focus had to change from development to dissemination; mass production, as he called it. At the same time, he ended the policy constraints he had imposed on the Institute for a long time. He removed the restriction not to use software or to consult for companies. He completed the full cycle he had started in 1983. The process of ongoing improvement became a three-legged approach, detailed as follows.

Education–Software–Support

With these three elements, and with the language, methodology and tools, Goldratt believed that he had delivered everything that was needed for the Institute to continue and disseminate and further develop TOC.

As he recognized that the organization had to go through a paradigm shift from development to mass production, he assumed that he could be a constraint to AGI and therefore, when he turned fifty, he retired from running the Institute.

Since his retirement on March 31, 1997, Goldratt has been devoting his time to things he likes to do. He further developed Project Management, especially in environments of multitudes of projects, and he intends to write more books. So far he has published six books. Three novels, *The Goal* (production), *Critical Chain* (project management and product development) and *It's Not Luck* (marketing and sales, Thinking Processes and day-to-day problems). The others are textbooks. *The Race* (Inventory and production), *The Haystack Syndrome* (decision-making and information systems), and *What Is This Thing Called Theory of Constraints and How Should It Be Implemented?* (a science-based approach to management).

Dr. Eli Goldratt's uniqueness is that he is a man who has been driven by his goal in life. He claims that it was clear to him when he was 20 that he would like to "teach the world to think." All his activities have been focused toward this goal. Goldratt's motto has ever been "I do not want to sacrifice anybody for my goal, but I will not sacrifice my goal for anybody." The lesson he wants to bring to people is "If you want to take your dreams seriously, use the TOC and work to make them come true."

Goldratt was born in Israel in 1947. He received his Ph.D. in Physics in 1975 from Bar-Ilan University, Israel. During his Ph.D. research in the flow of liquid he discovered an optimization process that could make him academically famous. He preferred not to publish it but to use it for business. The first opportunity came when he was asked to help in solving a production problem. This led him to use his formula in a scheduling software he called OPT. Even though he doesn't like to be called a genius or a guru, it is still amazing to watch his incredible capability in analyzing situations and inventing breakthrough solutions.

Citations

1) Preface to W. Edwards Deming, *The New Economics for Industry, Government, Education,* Massachusetts Institute of Technology for Advanced Engineering Study, Cambridge, Mass. (1993), p. xi.

2) Deming, *Out of the Crisis,* Massachusetts Institute of Technology for Advanced Engineering Study, Cambridge, Mass. (1982), p. 33.

3) *The New Economics for Industry, Government, Education,* p. 100.

4) Ibid., p. 134.

5) Ibid., p. 60.

6) Henry Neave, *The Deming Dimension,* SPC Press, Knoxville, Tenn. (1990), p. 124. Attributed to Joiner, B. L. and Scholtes, P. R. "Total Quality Leadership vs. Management by Control." Joiner Associates, Madison, Wis. (1985).

176	*Citations*

7) *The Deming Dimension*, p. 143.

8) Donald Wheeler, *Understanding Statistical Process Control*, SPC Press, Knoxville, Tenn. (1992), p. 4.

9) W. E. Shewhart, *Economic Control of Quality of Manufactured Product*, Van Nostrand, New York. (1931); reprinted by the American Society for Quality Control (1980), p. 6.

10) *Out of the Crisis*, pp. 248–275.

11) Stanislaw J. Lec *(The Quotations Homepage)*.

12) "W. Edwards Deming (1900–1993): The Man and His Message," British Deming Association, Salisbury, Wiltshire. (1997), p. 10.

13) Cecelia S. Kilian, *The World of W. Edwards Deming*, SPC Press, Knoxville, Tenn. (1992), p. 6.

14) *Doctor's Orders* (video). Central ITV, Birmingham, England (1988).

15) "Variation," no. 17, March 1994.

16) *The World of W. Edwards Deming*, pp. 176–7.

17) *If Japan Can . . . . Why Can't We?* Films Inc., Chicago, Ill.

18) "A visit . . . Modine, the McHenry Plant," *The Theory of Constraints Journal* vol. 1 (1987).

Bibliography

W. Edwards Deming

Out of the Crisis. Massachusetts Institute of Technology Center for Advanced Engineering Study, Cambridge, Mass. (1982).

The New Economics For Industry, Government, Education. Massachusetts Institute of Technology Center for Advanced Engineering Study, Cambridge, Mass. (1993).

Cecelia S. Kilian, *The World of W. Edwards Deming.* SPC Press, Knoxville, Tenn. (1992).

Henry Neave, *The Deming Dimension.* SPC Press, Knoxville, Tenn. (1990).

British Deming Association Booklets

A1 "A Brief History of Dr. W. Edwards Deming." British Deming Association, Salisbury, Wiltshire (1989).

A4 "Why SPC." British Deming Association, Salisbury, Wiltshire (1990).

A9 "A System of Profound Knowledge." British Deming Association, Salisbury, Wiltshire (1991).

A16 "How SPC." British Deming Association, Salisbury, Wiltshire (1990).

A17 "Flowcharting: How and Why?" British Deming Association, Salisbury, Wiltshire (1995).

A21 "W. Edwards Deming (1900–1993): The Man and his Message." British Deming Association, Salisbury, Wiltshire (1997).

Eliyahu M. Goldratt

What Is This Thing Called Theory of Constraints and How Should It Be Implemented? North River Press, Great Barrington, Mass. (1990).

The Haystack Syndrome: Sifting Information from the Data Ocean. North River Press, Great Barrington, Mass. (1990).

The Goal: A Process of Ongoing Improvement. North River Press, Great Barrington, Mass. (1992).

It's Not Luck. North River Press, Great Barrington, Mass. (1994).

Critical Chain. North River Press, Great Barrington, Mass. (1997).

The Theory of Constraints Journal. (vol. 1–6) Avraham Y. Goldratt Institute, 1987.

Walter A. Shewhart

Economic Control of Quality of Manufactured Product. Van Nostrand Company, Inc., New York (1931),; American Society for Quality Control (1980).

Statistical Method from the Viewpoint of Quality Control. Edited by W. Edwards Deming. Dover, Mineola, New York 1986.

Donald J. Wheeler

Four Possibilities. SPC Press, Knoxville, Tenn. (1983).

Understanding Statistical Precess Control. SPC Press, Knoxville, Tenn. (1992).

Understanding Variation. SPC Press, Knoxville, Tenn. (1994).

Advanced Topics in Statistical Process Control. SPC Press, Knoxville, Tenn. (1995).

Building Continual Improvement. SPC Press, Knoxville, Tenn. (1998).

General

Peter M. Senge, *The Fifth Discipline.* Doubleday, New York (1990).

Brian Joiner, *Fourth Generation Management.* McGraw Hill, Inc. New York (1994).

For further information visit
www.thedecalogue.com